A Guide To Tracing Your Limerick Ancestors

A Guide To Tracing Your Limerick Ancestors

Margaret Franklin

FLYLEAF PRESS

First published in 2003
Flyleaf Press
4 Spencer Villas
Glenageary
Co. Dublin, Ireland
www.flyleaf.ie

© 2003 Flyleaf Press

British Library cataloguing in Publication Data available

ISBN 0-9539974-4-8

Layout by Brian Smith

Cover illustration:
'The Treaty Stone Limerick'
by
Jacintha Walsh

Dedication

To

The memory of William Franklin of Doon South,
who traced so much by the fire and to Johnny
who encouraged me to write this down.

*'People will not look forward to posterity, who never look
backward to their ancestors.'*
- Edmund Burke 1729-1797 Irish philosopher and statesman.

Acknowledgements

I wish to acknowledge the direction and support of my editor Dr. James Ryan. I also wish to thank Dr. Christopher O'Mahony, Director of Limerick Archives for his helpful comments and suggestions. The staff of Limerick Ancestry particularly Margaret McBride were also most helpful. My thanks are also due to both Rosemary ffolliot and Mary Casteleyn who very graciously referred me to some family histories and transcriptions of parish registers. Tom Donovan helped with proof reading and Jacintha Walsh deserves mention for her sympathetic illustration. I would also like to thank Mary Guinan Darmody, Tim Cadogan and Peter Beirne of Tipperary, Cork and Clare libraries respectively. Thanks also to Christopher Barry of the planning /map department of Limerick County Council and Philip FitzGerald of Cappamore.. I would like finally to acknowledge the debt I owe to Limerick County and City Librarians present and past. Without them the collecting of local historical materials would be very much left to chance.

Table of Contents

Abbreviations Used

An. Hib.	Analecta Hibernica
Arch. Irel.	Archaeology Ireland
BL	British Library
BMD	Birth, marriage and death
c.	circa
CoI	Church of Ireland
CUP	Cork University Press
EM	Diocese of Cashel and Emly
FAS	Irish training authority
GO	Genealogical Office
GRO	General Register Office
IGRS	Irish Genealogical Research Society
IMC	Irish Manuscripts Commission
Ir.	Irish
Ir. Anc.	Irish Ancestor Journal
Ir Fam.Hist	Irish Family History Journal
Ir. Gen	Irish Genealogist Journal
JCHAS	Journal of the Cork Historical and Archaeological Society
Jrnl.	Journal
JRHAAI	Journal of the Royal Historical and Archaeological Association of Ireland
JRSAI	Journal of the Royal Society of Antiquaries of Ireland
KA	Kilbehenny/Anglesboro Parish Journal
KL	Diocese of Killaloe
LA	Limerick Ancestry
LC	Local Custody
LDS	Latter Day Saints Family History Library
LGDJ	Lough Gur and District Journal
LK	Diocese of Limerick
NAI	National Archives of Ireland
NLI	National Library of Ireland
NMAJ	North Munster Antiquarian Journal
NMunArch.Soc.Jrnl.	North Munster Archaeological Society Journal

n.d.	No date
OCM	O'Kief, Coshe Mang, Slieve Lougher and the Upper Blackwater in Ireland.(16 Vols)
OLJ	Old Limerick Journal
Pos.	Positive film
PRIA	Proceedings of the Royal Irish Academy
PRONI	Public Record Office Northern Ireland
RC	Roman Catholic
RCBL	Representative Church Body Library
SLC	Salt Lake City (i.e. Latter Day Saints)
THU	Tipperary Heritage Unit
UCC	University College Cork
UCD	University College Dublin
UJA	Ulster Journal of Archaeology

LIMERICK (County of), in the province of MUN-STER, bounded on the north by the estuary of the Shannon and the county of Tipperary ; on the east by the same county ; on the south by that of Cork, and on the west by that of Kerry : it extends from 52° 17' to 52° 45' (N. Lat.), and from 8° 6' to 9° 15' (W. Lon.) ; and comprises an area, according to the Ordnance survey, of 640,621 statute acres, of which 548,640 are cultivated land, and 91,981 are occupied by unimproved mountain and bog. The population, in 1821, was 218,432 ; and in 1831, 248,201.

Of the tribes mentioned by Ptolemy, the *Coriondi* appear to have inhabited this portion of Ireland ; and although from a very early period it was included in the native kingdom or principality of Thomond, it is said to have had at one time a separate political existence, under the name of *Aine-Cliach*, or *Eoganach-Aine-Cliach*, and to have been divided into five cantreds, governed by subordinate chieftains. That of Carrigoginniol belonged to the O'Kiarwicks, and afterwards to the O'Briens, whence the name of Pubblebrien was given to the barony ; Uaithney, now the barony of Owneybeg, belonged to the O'Ryans ; Cairbre Aobhdha, or Kenry, to the O'Donovans ; Hy-Cnocnuil-Gabhra, now the baronies of Upper Connello and Coshma, to the McEneirys and O'Sheehans ; and Connalla, now Lower Connello,
261

**From the *Topographical Dictionary of Ireland*
by Samuel Lewis (1837)**

Foreword

In this book an attempt is made to document the principal sources that are available for the study of Limerick ancestors. At the outset one should perhaps ask why trace roots at all. In Limerick today, families are experiencing an unprecedented economic boom. What therefore can a study of Limerick ancestors contribute to one's life? The answer is not altogether clear because the benefits of family history research are not, for the most part, measurable. The ultimate satisfaction gained may be a purely personal one. It is a satisfaction which does not require that the results of our study interest anyone else. This may be most true for those researching from abroad, where succeeding generations may be even more assimilated than the previous one and therefore less interested in their ancestry. Indeed lengthy research can often be ignored or discarded by the next generation. There are no guarantees that one's research will be recognized, rewarded or valued by whoever takes our place.

Having said all that we should point out that there are huge personal benefits to be reaped. Family history research involves piecing together a story from the remnants of surviving evidence of the lives of real people. It is a special story because it is our own story. Telling this story is an intellectual exercise that ultimately adds to our understanding of who we are and from where we have come.

The execution of this personal quest is not always easy. You must learn about the primary sources that are available for researching the past and how to use them. You must learn how to read documents, how to work on hunches and how to ferret out information from obscure sources. You will find yourself searching many different types of sources, often to no effect. Ultimately, however, you are on an educational learning curve about yourself and your past. One can learn to see beyond the present generation and come to understand how the present is shaped in a large measure by past events.

Tracing one's roots also leads to a personal understanding of the history of Limerick and Ireland. It is also central to understanding the history of our emigrants, the Irish Diaspora abroad. Limerick family history was shaped by national and local events: the confiscation and plantation of land in the seventeenth century; the Penal laws which impoverished the majority of the population; the Famine which caused the deaths of thousands and mass emigration of more to countries abroad. All of these events, and many other local events, affected Limerick families.

The study of family history is essentially centred around names. Most, if not all, family history would be impossible if the family name had not survived. Yet the lesson of history is that the name does survive, occasionally altered as a result of the effects of local accents or customs, but usually recognizable. This name, and the bloodlines it signifies, can link the researcher to families that have now adopted different cultures and often class backgrounds. It is hoped that this book stimulates a healthy intellectual curiosity about ancestors and that it in some way contributes to an enrichment of our understanding of family and society at home and abroad.

Chapter 1   Getting Started

Genealogy is the study of the descent of a family heir or head from a single ancestor. Family history is a wider study that fleshes out the skeleton that is produced by genealogists. It involves studying all members of ancestral families, rather than only direct descendants. It therefore involves acquiring an understanding of the historical circumstances in which one's ancestors lived. This allows us to gain a better understanding of the various contexts in which they lived; domestic, local and national.

In beginning the research of your Limerick ancestors the first thing to do is to develop a plan. You should think about which lines you want to follow. You have two parents, four grandparents and eight great-grandparents and so on. You cannot search all of these lines at once, so you need to define priorities in order to make your research more structured and feasible. You could therefore:

- Aim to produce a 'family tree' showing male-line ancestors and the wives, brothers and sisters of these.
- Decide on specific family lines (usually those with your own family name) and research all members back as far as you can trace.
- You could perhaps decide to compile an 'extended family tree'. In this you would show all the descendants (with their spouses) of some known ancestor.

However it is very advisable not to try to do it all together. It is best to concentrate on a small part of the tree at any one time. There are a number of blank pedigree charts available to organize your findings. The Church of Jesus Christ of the Latter Day Saints (LDS) Library, for example have produced many of these charts. Their PDF file on the internet is free and very useful. It can be downloaded from the Mormon LDS site (see chapter 13). There are also a number of genealogy software programs available on the internet; check www.cyndislist.com for a listing of what is currently on the market.

The usual research plan is to start with yourself and work backwards. You will fairly quickly have at least 8, if not 16, different family lines on which you could work. It is at this stage that you must make decisions as to where your priorities lie. On no account should you attempt to collect information on all lines in parallel. This will lead to confusion and inefficiencies.

In conducting research you must work from known family members to the lesser known and the unknown. In other words you must prove the link between definite members of your family and others. Presumption is not research. Talk or write to relatives, especially the older ones to get information on family members. Check to see what documents are available in the possession of the family. These might include letters, diaries, remembrance cards, newspaper cuttings, family prayer books etc. Establish the basic genealogical facts of your nearest relatives as best you can. These are the date and place of birth/baptism, marriage and death. Traditionally in Ireland ancestors were traced orally. This worked very well in small tight-knit communities where the oral tradition persisted. Sadly, however, many expert local genealogists died taking the trace with them, their vast store of knowledge undocumented.

It is very important to record the sources of your information as you progress along. Documentation is vitally important. Most family researchers experience the frustration of a recorded event in their files, but no recollection as to where it was obtained. Careful records of your searches will help your research and will also make your research available to others - even to coming generations. Computer programmes can be a great help in this process, although meticulous note-keeping by hand can be more appropriate in-situ.

The computer is useful not only in recording the facts of your search, but also in putting you in touch, via e-mail, with people the world over who may share your research interests. Remember to acknowledge your sources if you are making your research available on the internet.

If you are tracing your Limerick ancestors from abroad then research your family in your home country first. Many researchers know that their family came from Limerick, but do not know from which part. One search objective is therefore to find a record in your home country that will specify the part of Limerick from which your ancestors came. Passenger lists from Ireland are scarce, so arrival documentation in your home country may prove more useful. Surnames, particularly less common surnames, may also give a lead as certain surnames tended to be concentrated in particular areas.

Next familiarise yourself with the principal sources for Irish family research. The major archives are the National Archives of Ireland (NAI) and the National Library of Ireland (NLI). Access to national collections and archives is simplified by the websites of these institutions. They also set out guidelines on where to start research in these repositories (see chapter 13).

The major record types which you will almost certainly need to access include:
• Records of Birth, Marriage & Death (see Chapter 6: Civil Registration)
• Church Records (see Chapter 5: Church Records)

- Tithe Applotment Books (1820's – 1830's) (see chapter 3: Land Records)
- Griffith's Land Valuation (1852) (see chapter 3: Land Records)
- The censuses of 1901 and 1911 (see chapter 4:Census and Census substitutes)

Depending on the circumstances and local origin of your family, there may well be other sources that will prove useful. There are a number of current publications available that deal purely with genealogical research such as the *Irish Roots* magazine and the The *Irish Genealogist* journal. You should also avail of the expertise of your local librarian to connect you to sources elsewhere. For those who commission paid research make sure that you get professionals from reputable service providers.

Finally you should donate copies of your research to local libraries or heritage centres as these institutions gather this work for posterity and keep it in the public domain.

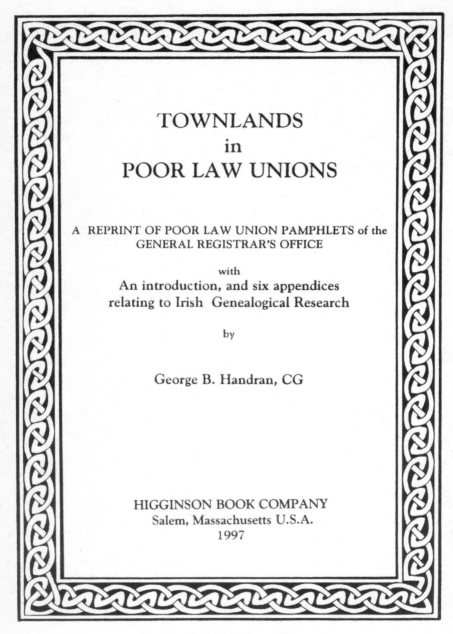

TOWNLANDS
in
POOR LAW UNIONS

A REPRINT OF POOR LAW UNION PAMPHLETS of the
GENERAL REGISTRAR'S OFFICE

with
An introduction, and six appendices
relating to Irish Genealogical Research

by

George B. Handran, CG

HIGGINSON BOOK COMPANY
Salem, Massachusetts U.S.A.
1997

Townlands in Poor Law Unions
edited by George B. Handran (Higginson Book Company, USA, 1997).

Chapter 2   Administrative Divisions

There are two systems of administration of which you should be aware. Land administration involves a series of land divisions (from province to townland), which are widely used in records. In addition, there is a system of administration originally developed to manage the Poor Law and since then used also for censuses, registration of births etc, and for elections. You will need to understand these administrative systems to conduct your research. However, it is not difficult to do so.

In land administration, Ireland is divided into the four **provinces** of Munster, Leinster, Ulster and Connaught. Within these provinces are 32 counties. The **county** is a major administrative division and many records are organised on a county basis. Within the county there are further administrative divisions. In this book we are only concerned with the county of Limerick.

Counties were historically divided into **baronies**, but these are little-used after the nineteenth century. As you can see from the map (see p.23) Limerick has 14 baronies. Baronies are an ancient land division, which are mainly relevant to early research. As certain records such as Griffith's Valuation are arranged by barony it can sometimes be important to establish in which one your ancestors lived. The *Index to Townlands*, (see below) will provide this information.

Baronies are further divided into **civil parishes**, which are units of considerable importance in the Irish administrative landscape. Note that these are civil parishes rather than parishes administered by the churches. You will come across many references to 'ecclesiastical parish,' 'Church of Ireland parish,' and 'Roman Catholic parish '. These are discussed below. Civil parishes are arguably the most important land division in Irish records as they are used for a huge range of administrative purposes. Finding the civil parish in which your ancestor lived is therefore an important objective of your preliminary research as land surveys are based on them.

The land within each parish is further subdivided into **townlands**. This unit may vary from 10 acres to several thousand acres and is the smallest official division of land. The biggest townlands tend to be those with the poor quality land. In general a townland will contain several hundred acres. It is important in defining the specific location of a family within the parish.

Boundaries of these ancient land divisions generally coincided with natural features of the landscape like streams, rivers or ridges. Sometimes manmade physical boundaries such as walls, hedges, roads or ditches formed the division. In recent years townland boundaries have become victims of the economic boom. Some of the features have disappeared as new roads and property are built. The changes in field size as a result of modern farm practice have also contributed to the blurring of distinctions between townlands.

The basic reference for administrative divisions is the *General Alphabetical Index to the Townlands and Towns , Parishes and Baronies of Ireland* or the *Index to Townlands*, as it is commonly known. It alphabetically lists all of the townlands in the country and provides the parish, barony and Poor Law Union in which each is located. It also lists all of the parishes and their location and gives the O.S. (Ordnance Survey) map reference for each townland.   This index was produced for the use of census enumerators every 10 years from 1821 to 1921. The 1851 edition of this book has been reprinted (Genealogical Publishing, Baltimore, 2000). It is widely available for consultation in libraries. You should also note that Y.M. Goblet's *1655-59 Index of Parishes & Townlands* (Dublin, IMC 1932) is useful if you are conducting research on 17th.century records. It is available in the National Library (ref. 9141gb) and in Limerick city and county Libraries.

Another useful reference work is George Handran's *Townlands in Poor Law Unions* (Higginson Book Co. Salem. Mass.1997), see page 16. It allows the reader to identify the names of all of the neighbouring townlands within a parish or union.

A second system of administration is less concerned with land, and more with the people on it. These administrative units started with the formation of **Poor Law Union** in the early nineteenth century. These unions were formed to administer the Poor Law, which was established in 1838 as a measure to relieve the poverty and hardship of the times through workhouses. Each Union was responsible for collecting a tax, and providing for the poor. The Poor Law Unions do not adhere to county and barony boundaries. For example, the Limerick unions stretched into east Clare, they were generally centred on a large town and were divided into **District Electoral Divisions** (D.E.D.'s). From the mid - nineteenth century onwards these became the units of administrative purpose. As other forms of administration were developed, they also used the same geographical areas. Thus they came to be used as the areas in which civil registration of births, marriages and deaths were conducted, in which elections were organised, and in which censuses were administered. As the 'cancelled books' of Griffiths Valuations (see next chapter) are arranged in order by D.E.D. (District Electoral Division) the listing of the townlands with the D.E.D. in Handran's work by Poor Law Union is a good aid to researchers.
The *General Alphabetical Index to the Townlands and Towns, Parishes and Baronies of Ireland* is very useful for these areas because it relates townlands

714   CENSUS OF IRELAND FOR THE YEAR 1851.

No. of Sheet of the Ordnance Survey Maps.	Townlands and Towns.	Area in Statute Acres.			County.	Barony.	Parish.	Poor Law Union in 1857.	Townland Census of 1851 Part I.	
		A.	R.	P.					Vol.	Page
11	Morerah	592	0	39	Leitrim	Drumahaire	Drumlease	Manorhamilton	IV.	
37, 38	Moress	316	3	1a	Donegal	Inishowen West	Inch	Londonderry	IV.	95
8, 9, 13 14	Morett	1,938	2	7	Queen's Co.	Portnahinch	Coolbanagher	Mountmellick	III.	121
113	Morgan's Island	0	3	32	Galway	Kiltartan	Kinvarradoorus	Gort	I.	244
10	Morgans North	807	0	23	Limerick	Connello Lower	Morgans	Rathkeale	IV.	50
									II.	228
10	Morgans South	405	0	36	Limerick	Connello Lower	Morgans	Rathkeale		
24	Morganstown	96	0	30	Kildare	Naas South	Kill	Naas	II.	228
18	Morganstown	82	1	28	Louth	Ferrard	Dysart	Drogheda	I	65
41	Mormeal	515	1	3	Londonderry	Loughinsholin	Kilcronaghan	Magherafelt	I	181
11	Mornane	751	3	25	Limerick	Kenry	Kilcornan	Rathkeale	III.	241
									II.	249
19, 23	Mornin	847	2	14	Longford	Moydow	Taghsheenod	Ballymahon	I.	162
21	Mornington	1,155	0	24	Meath	Lower Duleek	Colp	Drogheda	I.	195
21	MORNINGTON T.	—			Meath	Lower Duleek	Colp	Drogheda	I.	195
6, 7	Moroe	135	0	0	Limerick	Owneybeg	Abington	Limerick	II.	251
7	MOROE T.	—			Limerick	Owneybeg	Abington	Limerick	II.	251
6, 7	Moroewood	241	0	4	Limerick	Owneybeg	Abington	Limerick	II.	251
17	Moross	309	1	0	Donegal	Kilmacrenan	Clondavaddog	Milford	III.	125
25, 31	Morrell	204	1	6	Meath	Skreen	Kilcarn	Navan	I.	220
22	Morriscastle	246	0	28	Wexford	Ballaghkeen	Kilmuckridge	Gorey	I.	297
29	Morrissyland	26	2	16	Wexford	Bantry	St. Mary's	New Ross	I.	302
19	Morristown	101	3	1	Kildare	South Salt	Forenaghts	Naas	I.	77
23	Morristownbiller	435	1	14	Kildare	Connell	Morristownbiller	Naas	I.	56
18	Morristown Little	59	0	32ъ	Kildare	Connell	Oldconnell	Naas	I.	56
18	Morristown Lower	200	2	9c	Kildare	Connell	Oldconnell	Naas	I.	56
18, 23	Morristown Upper	332	0	26	Kildare	Connell	Oldconnell	Naas	I.	56
7	Mortarstown Lower	206	0	10d	Carlow	Carlow	Carlow	Carlow	I.	1
7	Mortarstown Upper	400	3	1 e	Carlow	Carlow	Carlow	Carlow	I.	1
22, 31	Mortgage	358	1	28	Limerick	Smallcounty	Fedamore	Croom	II.	259
37, 38, 40	Mortgage	148	2	39	Waterford	Decies within Drum	Kinsalebeg	Youghal	II.	352
19	Mortgage Fields	48	3	28	Kilkenny	Shillelogher	St. Patrick's	Kilkenny	I.	116
48, 56	Mortlestown	819	3	22	Limerick	Coshlea	Particles	Kilmallock	II.	240
76	Mortlestown	325	2	12	Tipperary, S.R.	Iffa and Offa West	Mortle-town	Clogheen	II.	319
54, 62	Mortle-town	754	3	2	Tipperary, S.R.	Middlethird	Cooleagh	Cashel	II.	326
76	Mortlestown Little	54	3	3b	Tipperary, S.R.	Iffa and Offa West	Mortlestown	Clogheen	II.	319
3	Moryclogh	285	0	26	Clare	Burren	Abbey	Ballyvaghan	II.	11
88	Mosestown	158	1	13	Cork, E.R.	Imokilly	Aghada	Middleton	II.	83
84, 96	Moskeagh	652	0	24	Cork, W.R.	Kinalmeaky	Templemartin	Bandon	II.	153
28	Mosney	200	3	15	Meath	Upper Duleek	Moorechurch	Drogheda	I.	198
91, 101	Mosshrook	371	1	19	Mayo	Clanmorris	Moyo	Claremorris	IV.	135
52	Mossfield	47	2	10	Donegal	Kilmacrenan	Gartan	Letterkenny	III.	127
38, 39	Mossfield	395	3	39	King's Co.	Ballybritt	Seirkieran	Parsonstown	I.	127
16	Mossfield or Urbal	238	3	19	Fermanagh	Tirkennedy	Trory	Enniskillen	III.	224
95, 96	Mos-grove	789	3	24	Cork, W.R.	Kinalmeaky	Templemartin	Bandon	II.	153
61	Mossmore	190	1	31	Tyrone	Dungannon Middle	Clonfeacle	Dungannon	III.	299
7, 8, 12, 13	Moss-side	284	2	24	Antrim	Cary	Grange of Drumtullagh	Ballycastle	III.	14
45	Moss-side	125	3	11	Antrim	Upper Antrim	Kilbride	Antrim	III.	14
7	MOSS-SIDE T.	—			Antrim	Cary	Grange of Drumtullagh	Antrim	III.	6
18, 22	Mosstown	183	2	22	Longford	Moydow	Kilcommock	Ballymahon	III.	14
22	Mosstown	491	2	4f	Longford	Rathcline	Kilcommock	Ballymahon	I.	161
24	Mosstown or Ballinkeeny	212	1	18	Westmeath	Rathconrath	Killare	Mullingar	I.	164
									I.	283
24	Mosstown Demesne	140	0	3	Westmeath	Rathconrath	Killare	Mullingar	I.	283
18	Mosstown North	234	3	14g	Louth	Ardee	Mosstown	Ardee	I.	174
18	Mosstown South	52	3	9	Louth	Ardee	Mosstown	Ardee	I.	174
13	Mossy Glen	793	1	25	Donegal	Inishowen East	Moville Lower	Inishowen	III.	119
12, 13	Mustragee	300	0	39	Antrim	Lower Dunluce	Derrykeighan	Ballymoney	III.	17
6, 9	Mota	201	0	20	Tipperary, N.R.	Lower Ormond	Kilbarron	Borrisokane	II.	284
26	Motabeg or Salville	140	0	2b	Wexford	Ballaghkeen	Templeshannon	Enniscorthy	II.	299
5, 6	Motalower	325	3	12	Wexford	Gorey	Templeshannon	Shillelagh	I.	316
41	M tulee	344	1	33	Londonderry	Loughinsholin	Desertmartin	Magherafelt	III.	240
40, 41, 42	Mote Demesne	1,263	3	3	Roscommon	Athlone	Kilmeane	Roscommon	IV.	182
3, 7	Mothel	259	1	21	Waterford	Upperthird	Mothel	Carrick on Suir	II.	371
25	Mough	175	2	38	Leitrim	Leitrim	Fenagh	Mohill	IV.	100
16, 24	Mough or Greatwood	132	3	20	King's Co.	Ballyboy	Kilbughy	Tullamore	II.	124
34	Moughley	42	0	23	Fermanagh	Magherastephana	Aghalurcher	Lisnaskea	III.	217
99, 100	Moularostig	195	2	30	Kerry	Dunkerron South	Kilcrohane	Kenmare	II.	184
37, 40, 41	Mouler-town or Bally voulera	321	1	26	Kilkenny	Ida	Kilcoan	Waterford	I.	102
50	Mount	138	2	3	Clare	Clonderalaw	Kilchreest	Killadysert	III.	15
61	Mountain	66	2	27	Galway	Clonmacnowen	Ahascragh	Ballinasloe	IV.	24
98	Mountain	81	3	30	Galway	Kilconnell	Killallaghtan	Ballinasloe	IV.	41
93	Mountain	221	1	23h	Mayo	Costelio	Bekan	Claremorris	IV.	139

(a) Including 8A. 1R. 21P. reclaimed land.　(d) Including 9A. 0R. 16P. River Barrow.　(g) Including 13A. 3R. 8P. water.
(b) Including 2A. 2R. 11P. water.　(e) Including 14A. 3R. 5P. River Barrow.　(h) Including 38A. 1R. 8P. water.
(c) Including 5A. 1R. 20P. water.　(f) Including 14A. 2R. 16P. water.

A page from the 'General Alphabetical Index to the Townlands and Towns, Parishes and Baronies of Ireland' based on the census of Ireland for the year 1851

and civil parishes to a specific Poor Law Union. The 1901 edition also gives the (D.E.D.) name and number. These are important if you are attempting to search the 1901 or 1911 census (see Chapter 4).

The final systems of administration are those of the **churches**. In this context it is important to know that the **Church of Ireland** was not simply another religion. Until the late 19th century, it was the Established Church and as such was very much an arm of government and wielded considerable power. It collected a local tax called a tithe, it proved Wills within its own court system, and registered burials. This is further discussed in later chapters.

The **Roman Catholic** parish is sometimes equivalent in area to the civil parish but usually not. A single Catholic parish may include more than one civil parish, or one civil parish may cover parts of several different Catholic parishes.

COLEMAN'S WELL, or CLOUNCORAGH, a parish, in the barony of UPPER CONNELLO EAST, county of LIMERICK, and province of MUNSTER, 2 miles (N. N. W.) from Charleville, on the road to Ballingarry; containing 821 inhabitants. This parish comprises 4506 statute acres, as applotted under the tithe act. It is watered by the river Maigue, which here forms a boundary between the counties of Cork and Limerick. The land in every part is moderately good, and in the neighbourhood of Foxall and Drewscourt, where it is well farmed and planted, it is very fertile; the meadow land is considered equal to any in the county. The living is a rectory, in the diocese of Limerick, and held in commendam by the Bishop, or, according to some writers, forms part of the mensal of the see : the tithes amount to £110. 0. 10. The church has long since fallen into decay, and the Protestant parishioners attend divine service in the parish church of Bruree. In the R. C. divisions the parish forms part of the union or district of Bruree, which is also called Rockhill, and contains a chapel. The water of St. Colman's well is reputed to possess great efficacy, and is held in high veneration by the peasantry of the surrounding country who assemble here in great numbers on the anniversary of the saint, and at other times.

A description of the Civil Parish of Coleman's Well from the
Topographical Dictionary of Ireland **by Samuel Lewis(1837).**

For example this is the case with the Catholic parish of Doon which includes parts of the civil parishes of Oola, Cappamore (Tuogh) and even Murroe. Also note from the map of the Roman Catholic parishes that the parishes of Parteen and Cratloe are in Co. Clare, though in Limerick diocese.

Both Church of Ireland and Roman Catholic parishes are grouped into dioceses. The Catholic dioceses are Limerick, Killaloe and Cashel and Emly. There is also one civil parish, Kilbolane, which is in the Cork diocese of Cloyne. The Church of Ireland parishes are similar to civil parishes but are not coterminous.

There are also a number of other placename or geographical reference sources which are essential tools for family and local area research in Co. Limerick. *The Topographical Dictionary of Ireland* by Samuel Lewis was first published in 1837. This contains a wealth of local historical and contemporary information on the villages, market towns, the city and the dioceses of Limerick (see p.10). It is particularly useful because it relates the individual civil parish to the corresponding Roman Catholic parish. It also gives the location of churches. This book comes in two volumes with a set of 32 county maps and has recently been reprinted by De Burca books (Dublin). The Limerick entries in Lewis are now available at the Limerick County Council website *www.lcc.ie* Click on 'library' then 'local studies' then 'online publication'.

The Parliamentary Gazetteer of Ireland for 1844/5 (Dublin, A. Fullerton, 1846) is like Lewis's work in content and arrangement. It can help to locate and validate a placename encountered in research.

Another series that aids local research is the **Field Name Books** which were the notebooks compiled by John O'Donovan when surveying the county for the first ordnance survey maps in 1838-40. They give the townland names in Irish and English, the derivation of the names and their location within the parish (see p. 25). The original transcripts are kept in the National Library of Ireland, but copies i.e. typed transcripts are also in local custody (Limerick City and County Libraries).

Map No.	Civil Parish	Tithe Applotments	Map No.	Civil Parish	Tithe Applotments
74	Abbeyfeale	1829-31	20	Doondonnell	1828
61	Abington	1826	90	Drehidtarsna	1826
89	Adare	1827	97	Dromin	1833
60	Aglishcormick	1826	58	Dromkeen	1832
93	Anhid	1833	85	Dromcolliher	1827
11	Ardagh	1826	7	Dunmoylan	1833
27	Ardcanny	1833	92	Dysert	1833
121	Ardpatrick	1834	102	Effin	1829
14	Askeaton	1827	117	Emlygreennan	1832
95	Athlacca	1834	104	Fedamore	1826
116	Athneasy	1824	120	Galbally	1830
109	Ballinard	1834	105	Glenogra	1835
122	Ballingaddy	1832	72	Grange	1830
81	Ballingarry(Con)	1826	65	Grean	1834
125	Ballingarry(Cos)	1830	100	Hackmys	1833
111	Ballinlough	1833	112	Hospital	1834
57	Ballybrood	1827	56	Inch St.Lawrence	1833
38	Ballycahane	1825	24	Iveruss	1828
126	Ballylanders	1829	130	Kilbeheny	1826/30
66	Ballynaclogh	1832	88	Kilbolane	1830-31
110	Ballynamona	1833	9	Kilbradran	1833
119	Ballyscaddan	1833	115	Kilbreedy Major	1834
96	Bruff	1833	101	Kilbreedy Minor	1833
84	Bruree	1827-34	8	Kilcolman	1830
50	Cahervally	1826	25	Kilcornan	1825
53	Caherconlish	1825-27	108	Kilcullane	1833
106	Cahercorney	1833	28	Kildimo	1825
55	Caherelly	1833	2	Kilfergus	1830
51	Cahernarry	1825	124	Kilfinane	1831
17	Cappagh	1828	79	Kilfinny	1834
49	Carrigparson	1826	128	Kilflyn	1829
64	Castletown	1826	113	Kilfrush	1833
26	Chapelrussel	1825	29	Kilkeedy	1833
19	Clonagh	1830	78	Killagholehane	1828
80	Cloncagh	1833	77	Killeedy	1832
86	Cloncrew	1834	30	Killeely	1833
73	Clonelty	1833	43	Killeengarriff	1827-32
47	Clonkeen	1831	37	Killeenoghty	1826
18	Clonshire	1831	34	Killonahan	1825
87	Colmanswell	1828	82	Kilmeedy	1827
83	Corcomohide	1829	6	Kilmoylan	1833
35	Crecora	1827	42	Kilmurry	1833
22	Croagh	1825	103	Kilpeacon	1826
91	Croom	1826/28 31	127	Kilquane	1834
129	Darragh	1831	23	Kilscannell	1827
46	Derrygalvin	1833	69	Kilteely	1826
48	Donoghmore	1825	107	Knockaney	1833
63	Doon	1826	118	Knocklong	1834

Map No. Civil Parish	Tithe Applotments	Map No. Civil Parish	Tithe Applotments
36 Knocknagaul	1825	71 Newcastle	1829
Limerick City:		68 Oola	1826
1 St. John	*1833*	123 Particles	1833
44 St. Lawerence	*n/a*	59 Rathjordan	1833
1 St. Mary	*n/a*	21 Rathkeale	1825
33 St. Michael	*1828*	10 Rathronan	1833
31 St. Munchin	*1825*	5 Robertstown	1833
45 St. Nicholas	*1826*	54 Rochestown	1833
41 St. Patrick	*1824/27*	114 St. Peter & Paul	1830
15 Lismakeery	1827	4 Shanagolden	1830
3 Loughill	1832	40 Stradbally	1827/29/32
52 Ludden	1826	99 Tankardstown	1834
76 Mahoonagh	1833	70 Templebredon	1826/34
75 Monagay	1828	13 Tomdeely	1830
39 Monasteranenagh	1826/1834	94 Tullabracky	1833
12 Morgans	1833	62 Tuogh	1826
32 Mungret	1822/25/27	67 Tuoghcluggin	1827
16 Nantinan	1829	98 Urgare	1833

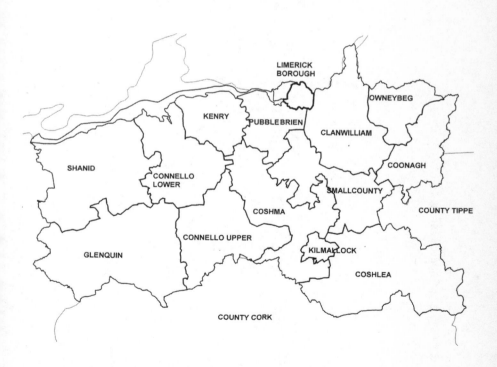

Barony Map of County Limerick

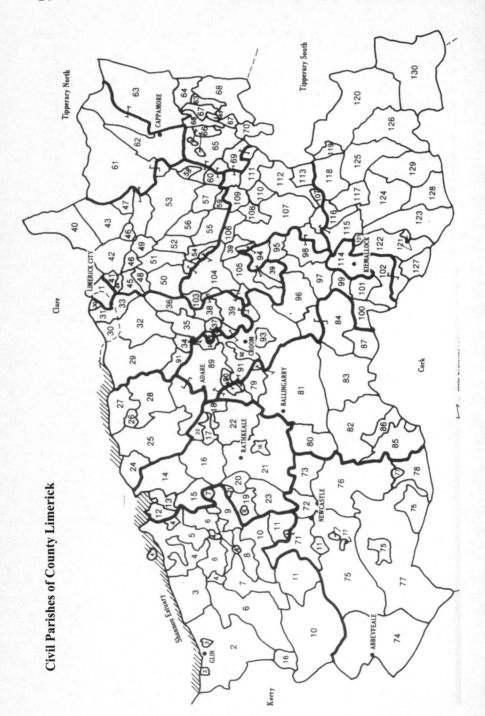

Civil Parishes of County Limerick

59

Finneterstown (contd.)

Finneterstown	-- Revd. Richd. Maunsell, Rector.
Finneterstown	-- Presentment Book for 1839.
Finmitterstowne	-- Down Survey
Finiterstown	-- Acts of Settmt. &c. 1666-1684.
Binnitterstowne	-- Down Survey
Finiterstown	-- Acts of Settmt. &c.

Situated in the South of the Parish of Drehidtrasna Barony of Connello Upper and County of Limerick. 21.

The property of Anthony Butler St. Leger, agent Pelham Babbington Arthurstown County Wexford, let to 7 tenants from four of whom have leases of 21 years and 3 are tenants at will, rent from 15s. to 30s. per acre. County Cess per acre from 2/8 to 3/6. Size of farms from 6 to 40 acres. Soil light and gravelly, producing wheat, oats and potatoes, fuel scarce, prevailing names Hogan and Hartigan. Authy. G. Sullivan, a tenant.

Glebe of Drehidtrasna   -- By. Surveyor's Sketch 6

See Parish name.   J.O'D.

Glebe of Drehidtrasna   -- Revd. Richd. Maunsell, Rector.

- Situated in the South of the Parish of Drehidtrasna Barony of Coshma and County of Limerick.

The property of Lord George Quin, England, agent Thos. Disney Junr. Esq. Dublin, let to the Revd. Richd. Maunsell during his life at £22. for townland. County Cess 2/6 to 3/6 tithe 19s. 6d. Soil heavy, usual crops wheat, oats, & potatoes. Fuel scarce, prevailing names O'Dea, and Maunsell. There is a Glebe House here two stories high - built in 1816 with a plain garden, and a good set of offices.
Authy: Revd. Richd. Maunsell, Glebe.

Glebe House of Drehidtarsna   -- Revd. Richd. Maunsell   7

See Parish name.   J.O'D.

Situated in the Townland of Glebe of Drehidtrasna in the Parish of Drehidtrasna and County of Limerick.

A page from the Ordnance Survey Field Name Book for Limerick

GRANTOR	GRANTEE	County, City, or Corporation Town in which any of the Premises granted are situate.	General Charge	Year of Registry	Number of Plea Side Volume / Office Copy Abstract Book	Number of Folio of Plea Side Vol. / File in the Office copy Abstract Book
Hannagton, Eliza {for several Grantors}	Blackwood Wm S. Stern & Rent	Tyrone Co		1857	14	87
Rev James C.	King Robert	Tyrone Co		1854	13	184
Hannahan, Anne née Hannan	Joseph Vant	Limerick City	9. 1851		14	156
Bridget for	Barnes Thomas	Tipperary Co		1854	7	167
Bridget for	Fox John	Tipperary Co		1856	13	115
Bryan	Stein Jameson	Limerick City		1854	16	160
Bryan	Clifford Hannah	Limerick City		1857	16	269

A sample page from the Grantor's Index to Deeds held at the Registry of Deeds. A microfilm copy of the indexes is available at the NLI. (see p.28)

Chapter 3   Land Records

During the eighteenth century and most of the   nineteenth century the
occupiers of Irish land were rarely its owners. They were small farmers and
cottiers who rented or leased the land from large estates which were almost
all owned by English and Anglo-Irish landlords. The terms of occupancy of
these lands was a major political issue. Most small tenants were 'tenants at
will', i.e. they could be evicted on the decision of the landlord. Even some of
the larger landholders held their land on the basis of agreements that were not
documented. The struggle to acquire better terms of tenure for land was one of
the great political battles that was played out locally and nationally throughout
the last quarter of the nineteenth century.

As comprehensive census returns are not available, the surviving land records,
whether surveys or rentals have become a very important source in tracing
families. The principal surviving Limerick land records are:

- The Civil Survey of 1654-56
- Records of the Registry of Deeds 1708-to date
- Tithe Applotment Survey 1823-37
- Griffith's Valuation 1851-52
- Estate Records
- Land Registry 1897 to date

Civil Survey of 1654 - 56
This survey was carried out to survey the lands confiscated by the English
Crown following the 1641 rebellion. The English parliament ordered many of
the people surveyed to leave county Limerick.
Huge areas of land were confiscated and redistributed to the adventurers
and soldiers who supported the Crown. Those transplanted were issued
with Transplantation Certificates in 1653. These certificates give the age,
wife and children of those concerned. This information has been published
in 2000 in the article 'Cromwellian Transplantation from Limerick, 1653'
by S. C. O'Mahony in NMAJ, 40, p. 29-51. This survey records the old and
new landowners, and the place names of the county. Related information is
contained within the Books of Survey and Distribution compiled c.1703 which
lists proprietors of land in 1641 and the grantees of 1666-68 i.e. those who
were granted these lands at various times in the second half of the seventeenth
century. This is held in the National Library of Ireland and also the Royal Irish
Academy (see next chapter and chapter 13).

Registry of Deeds 1708 -
A deed is simply a written agreement, which can involve one or more people and can theoretically be on any subject. From 1708 deeds had to be lodged in the 'Registry of Deeds' in Dublin. What was registered however, was not the deed itself but an abbreviated copy, known as a 'memorial'. The original memorials have been kept but what is available to the public are transcripts bound in huge volumes. Photographic reproductions of the originals are available on request. Any type of agreement could be the subject of a deed, but the vast bulk of those registered concern land lease, sale, conveyance or mortgage. They also concern marriage settlements, name changes and other unusual forms of agreement, which can often be of great family history significance. The genealogically important information contained in an average deed includes the date, names, addresses and occupations of the parties to the deed, the family circumstances disclosed by the details of the agreement and the names, addresses and occupations of the witnesses.

Some historians would contend that the Registry of Deeds was set up primarily to secure Protestant control of land ownership. Catholics had little access to legal assistance within the courts during the 18th century. Imposition of increased legal process on land ownership was therefore one of many ways in which it was made more difficult for Catholics to retain, or gain, control of land. It was not until 1778 that Catholics could inherit in the same way as Protestants. However, the vast bulk of deeds concern large landholdings. If one's ancestor was a smallholder there is little chance of finding a deed especially as registration was voluntary. This applies particularly to the eighteenth century. The use of deeds for land transactions was also locally variable. Some estates and communities used them, while others, such as the Quaker community, and Palatine families, were infrequent users.

Researching in the Registry of Deeds can be quite a daunting task and may very well be a job for the seasoned researcher. Finding your way through the indexing system can be confusing; the volumes are physically heavy; and the text of deeds can contain legal jargon and abbreviations which may be difficult to understand. Readers are recommended to look at Rosemary ffolliott's article 'The Registry of Deeds for Genealogical Purposes' in *Irish Genealogy – A Record Finder* (Heraldic Artists, Dublin 1987) for an excellent introduction to this topic.

There are two sets of indexes that can be used to locate deeds - a Grantor's index and a Land index. The grantor index lists those selling (or otherwise 'granting') the land (see p.26), while the Land index lists the properties being transferred. There is no index to Grantees, i.e. those buying, renting or otherwise receiving the land. The land index is arranged by county. These indexes do not cover the entire period as a single unit but are a series of indexes in which consecutive periods are covered.

The LDS have filmed the entire contents of the names index on 122 reels and the land index on 283 reels. Copies of these films have been deposited in the NLI. So instead of having to check the original indexes you have now this option, which can be carried out at a more leisurely pace. You should also check out the website of the Registry of Deeds (see p.110) as this gives a good outline of the functions of the office and the types of searches that can be made (see chapter 13).

As support material for the verification of deeds, many wills were also submitted to the Registry of Deeds. The Irish Manuscripts Commission has published a three volume summary of these wills up to 1832. This contains a full index to persons and places. The details are:

Registry of Deeds, Dublin: Abstracts of Wills –
• Vol. I 1708-45 (IMC, Dublin 1954) edited by P.B. Eustace
• Vol. II 1746-85 (IMC, Dublin 1956) edited by P.B. Eustace
• Vol. III 1785-1832 (IMC, Dublin 1984) edited by E. Ellis and P.B. Eustace.

Tithe Applotment Survey 1823-37
A tithe was a church tax used for the upkeep of the Church of Ireland clergymen in each parish. It was based on an estimate of the produce by each landholder. As the Church of Ireland was the state or Established church, members of all churches had to pay this tax. This caused considerable resentment among other denominations as only about ten percent of the population belonged to the Church of Ireland. The payment of the tithe was further exacerbated by the fact that from 1736 grazing land was made exempt from tithes. As grazing lands were owned predominantly by landlords this fuelled more resentment.
Originally the tithes could be paid 'in kind', i.e. by contribution of farm products to the local minister. However, from the 1820s a cash payment was required. In order to bring about this change all agricultural land had to be surveyed and valued (apploted) so as to determine the amount payable by each landholder. This was carried out by local surveyors from 1823-37. The surveyors assessed the average income that could be expected from each piece of land in each townland.

The results were compiled into parish Tithe Applotment Books, listing the landholders and the tithe payable by each. These books are not a comprehensive survey of householders as they do not include those who lived in towns or landless labourers. They are however the first register of all landholders in Ireland. They can tell you about the type and amount of land owned by your ancestors. The Tithe books are valuable for this period when few other records survive. In Munster, tithes were payable on potato patches and not on grassland with the result that the poorest had to pay the most. A significant advantage of the Tithe books is that they list landholders for the period before the Famine and are therefore a very important source for this critical period.

After the Catholic Emancipation Act in 1829, a movement for the elimination of the tithes began. In the 1830s there was widespread refusal to pay the tithes and so-called 'tithe wars' occurred sporadically throughout the country. A celebrated refusal to pay the tithe occurred in Doon, Co. Limerick. The local priest, Fr.Hickey had his cow seized in lieu of payment. For a more detailed account of this event see Mark Tierney's book *Murroe and Boher* (Browne & Nolan, Dublin, 1966.) Such confrontations occurred widely in Ireland at the time. The refusal to pay tithes reduced many of the parochial clergy of the Established Church to poverty. As a result, those affected by non-payment could apply for state assistance under legislation passed in 1832. The clergy had to draw up a list of those who defaulted on payment of the tithe. This list gave the defaulter's place of residence, their occupation and the amount due. There is a defaulter's list for Co. Limerick but it is not comprehensive. By 1838 tithes were reduced by twenty five percent and the onus was on the landlord to pay them.This was to see their virtual abolition and they were legally abolished in 1869.

The Tithe Applotment Books are available on microfilm at local Limerick libraries and at Limerick Ancestry where they have been indexed (see Chapter 13). The tithe books were not compiled according to a standard format. Some are very uniform and legible while others may be vague and illegible. A 'Surname only' index to the tithe applotments for Limerick can be found within the surname index to the Griffiths Valuations (see below).

The original tithe books are held in the NAI. The Representative Church Body Library(RCBL) has a cess applotment book for Abington, Co.Limerick 1823-24 (ms. 1-2). The NLI ms. 16085 is the personal note-book of Edmund Sexten c.1590-1630, which contains estimates of the tithes due by named tenants on various estates in Co.Limerick.

Griffith's Valuation 1851-52

The General Valuation of Rateable Property in Ireland is more often known as *Griffith's Valuation* after the surveyor and engineer Richard Griffith who first carried it out. Because it was the first, it is also known as the Primary Valuation. It was a survey of all the land and property in Ireland carried out in order to determine the amount of rates (local taxes) each occupier must pay on their property for local administrative purposes. The valuation was published in printed volumes and arranged by county, barony, poor law union, parish and townland. Like most towns and cities, Limerick City is arranged by civil parish, and within each parish, by street, and sometimes by ward.

This valuation is an important source because it recorded almost every head of household in Ireland in the period immediately after the Famine. Nationwide it documents those who occupied land from approximately 1848 onwards. The start date for the Valuation varies from county to county, for obvious practical reasons. The Limerick Valuation was completed in the 1850-52 period. It recorded the size of holdings and the valuation, based on an estimate of the land's productive capacity. The information contained can give an indication

PRIMARY VALUATION OF TENEMENTS,

PARISH OF DOON.

No. and Letters of Reference to Map.	Names. Townlands and Occupiers.	Immediate Lessors.	Description of Tenement.	Area.	Net Annual Value. Land.	Buildings.	Total.
	KILMOYLAN, UP. —continued.			A. R. P.	£ s. d.	£ s. d.	£ s. d.
8	George Franklin, Patrick Lonergan,	Court of Chancery,	Land,	5 0 33	2 15 0 / 2 15 0	—	2 15 0 / 2 15 0
9 A B	Richard Hayes,	Court of Chancery,	Land,	0 3 28 / 9 2 2	0 16 0 / 6 4 0	—	7 0 0
10 a	Richard Hayes,	Court of Chancery,	House, offices, and land,	38 0 8	27 0 0	4 0 0	31 0 0
11 A B a	John Keogh,	Court of Chancery,	House and land, Land,	22 2 0 / 23 0 31	14 15 0 / 16 18 0	1 2 0	32 15 0
12	Sarah Lonergan,	Court of Chancery,	House, offices, and land,	4 2 4	11 10 0	1 5 0	12 15 0
13 a	Thomas Hammersley,	Court of Chancery,	House and land,	2 0 0	1 4 0	0 11 0	1 15 0
14 a	David Lonergan,	Court of Chancery,	House, office, and land,	7 3 4	5 2 0	0 18 0	6 0 0
			Total,	246 3 37	171 10 0	12 16 0	184 6 0
	KNOCKNACARRIGA (Ord. S. 15.)						
1 a	Rev. Thos. Atkinson,	Ecclesiastel. Commis.	House, offices, and land, Orchard,	47 1 19	41 0 0	31 0 0	72 0 0 / 4 0 0
b	John Falry,	Rev. Thos. Atkinson,	House and garden,	0 0 33	0 3 0	2 7 0	2 10 0
2 A B	Rev. Thos. Atkinson,	Trus.E.Smith'sCharities	Land,	11 0 12 / 53 3 18	7 15 0 / 29 10 0		37 5 0
3 a	John Ryan,	Michael Cunningham,	House, offices, and land,	8 3 39	6 0 0	0 15 0	6 15 0
4 A B a	Michael Cunningham,	Trus.E.Smith'sCharities	House, office, and land, Land,	2 1 29 / 1 1 35	1 10 0 / 1 0 0	2 5 0	4 15 0
a	William Shanalan,	Michael Cunningham,	House,			0 13 0	0 13 0
5 a	John Spelman,	Michael Cunningham,	House and land,	1 1 21	1 2 0	0 12 0	1 14 0
6 a	John Mockler,	Michael Cunningham,	House and land,	1 3 14	1 12 0	1 3 0	2 15 0
7	Trus.E.Smith'sCharities	In fee,	Bog,	123 3 31			100 0 0
			Total,	252 2 11	89 12 0	38 15 0	232 7 0
	KYLEGARVE, (Ord. S. 15 & 16.)						
1 a	John Ryan (Luke),	H. M. O'Grady, Esq.	House and land,	30 1 23	15 2 0	0 13 0	15 15 0
b	Honoria Costelloe,	John Ryan (Luke), jun.	House and garden,	0 0 15	0 2 0	0 9 0	0 11 0
2	James Morrison,	H. M. O'Grady, Esq.	Land,	1 2 32	0 9 0	—	0 9 0
3 A B	H. M. O'Grady, Esq.	In fee,	Bog, Land,	45 0 32 / 5 2 24	1 15 0	—	50 0 0 / 1 15 0
A a	John Hayes,	H. M. O'Grady, Esq.	House,		—	0 10 0	0 10 0
b	Patrick Fogarty,	H. M. O'Grady, Esq.	House,		—	0 10 0	0 10 0
4 a	James Ryan,	H. M. O'Grady, Esq.	House, office, and land,	14 3 2	5 0 0	0 15 0	5 15 0
5 a	John Ryan (Luke)	H. M. O'Grady, Esq.	House, office, and land,	30 2 31	8 6 0	0 14 0	9 0 0
b	Thomas Mulcahy,	John Ryan (Luke),	House,		—	0 8 0	0 8 0
6 a	Patrick Connor	H. M. O'Grady, Esq.	House, offices, and land,	25 1 22	11 10 0	0 15 0	12 5 0
7 a	Jeremiah Bray,	H. M. O'Grady, Esq.	House, offices, and land,	38 0 28	8 2 0	0 18 0	9 0 0
8 A B a	John Doherty,	H. M. O'Grady, Esq.	House and land, Land,	38 2 22 / 2 0 8	8 18 0 / 1 0 0	0 12 0	10 10 0
9 a	William Ryan,	H. M. O'Grady, Esq.	House, offices, and land,	18 2 37	6 14 0	1 1 0	7 15 0
10 a	John Ryan (William)	H. M. O'Grady, Esq.	House, office, and land,	15 0 31	5 15 0	1 0 0	6 15 0
11 a	Mary Ryan,	H. M. O'Grady, Esq.	House, office, and land,	44 1 6	13 10 0	2 0 0	15 10 0
			Total,	320 3 36	86 3 0	10 5 0	146 8 0
	LACKABEG, (Ord. S. 16.)						
1	Patrick Walsh,	H. M. O'Grady, Esq.	Land,	64 2 20	20 0 0	—	20 0 0
a	John Carney,	Patrick Walsh,	House and garden,	0 0 24	0 1 0	0 12 0	0 13 0
b	Timothy Hickey,	Patrick Walsh,	House,		—	0 6 0	0 6 0
a	Judith Ryan,	Patrick Walsh,	House and garden,	0 0 39	0 2 0	0 10 0	0 12 0
2 a	Patrick Ryan,	Patrick Walsh,	House and land,	3 0 3	0 17 0	0 9 0	1 6 0

A page from *Griffiths Primary Valuations*
which were carried out in Limerick in 1851-52

of an ancestor's socio-economic status

The kind of information one is likely to discover in Griffith's includes the following:

☐ Name of occupier
☐ Name of immediate lessor (or landlord)
☐ Description of the property e.g., house, offices (barns/sheds)
☐ Description of land (garden, bog, mountain etc.).
☐ Area of the land in acres, roods and perches.
☐ Rateable annual value of the land and buildings (separate valuations)
☐ Total valuation.

If one checks the Rate Revision Books held in the Valuation Office (Abbey St. Lower, Dublin) or the microfilms held by the Mormon Latter Day Saints (LDS)library one can follow the history of a property's occupancy and eventual ownership right up to about 1930 (see chapter 13 for LDS library details).
A useful aid when using Griffith's is the Index of Surnames compiled by the National Library of Ireland. This is a typed index to all of the householders names listed. It is sometimes also called the 'Householders Index'. The index covers not only Griffith's but also the Tithe Applotment Survey. This index is divided into two sections. The first section gives an alphabetical list of surnames stating the baronies in which each occurs. The second part is divided into baronies and is an alphabetical list of names within each civil parish. The initial 'G' after a name indicates that a householder of this name appears in Griffith's and the initial 'T' indicates an occurrence in the Tithe Applotment Survey. The number of householders with each name is indicated, but only for the Griffith Valuation. The index is thus very useful as it can indicate the frequency of a surname in an area. Photocopies and microfilm of this index are widely available both locally in the NAI and LDS. Eneclann have also produced a complete edition of Griffith's Valuation for Ireland on CD-ROM. All available copies of the valuation (published over the 17 years it took to complete) are indexed. See *www.eneclann.ie* for details.

Also in existence are the notebooks, (Field Books, House Books and Tenure Books), used by the surveyors to record details of the lands and properties surveyed. The House Books give details about the dwelling and out-buildings on a holding. The Tenure Books detail whether the holding was leased or if the holder was a tenant at the will of the landlord. These books may yield information needed to find a deed at the registry of deeds. These notebooks are held in the NAI. They are arranged by county, barony, parish and townland. As time passed the changes in the ownership of holdings had to be recorded to update the original valuation. When ownership changed the new occupier was written in. Usually a pen of a different colour ink was used. These changes make up what are known as the '*cancelled books*' and are held by the Valuation

Office, Dublin.
Copies of the Griffith Valuation are widely available in libraries. The maps which accompanied the valuation are now on CD-ROM (produced by the Valuation Office) a disk of which is held by Limerick County Library. Useful additional information on landowners can be found in:
'Return of owners of Land of 1 acre and upwards ...in Ireland' first pub 1876. (reprinted: Genealogical Pub. Co.1988).
O.H. Hussey de Burgh's *Landowners of Ireland*, gives the names of proprietors of all properties over 500 Acres (or £500 valuation) in 1878. This is available for consultation in the NLI.

Estate Records
Large holdings of land, which were leased or rented to tenants, were known as estates. Many, if not most, of these estates have no existing records of their tenants. Where they exist, however, estate records can provide information on the tenants, rents charged, employee wage books and tenancy maps. In order to locate these records one must first identify the estate owner. One can do this by checking Griffith's and or the *'Persons'* or *'Places'* volume of the index to Hayes' *Manuscript Sources for the History of Irish Civilisation* published by G. K. Hall, Boston, Mass. 1965. This 11 volume work lists the manuscripts held by the major repositories of Irish material in Ireland and the UK, and some US libraries. There is also a three-volume supplement to Hayes' which was published in 1979. One other useful finding aid is *A Catalogue of Irish Manuscripts in the National Library of Ireland* published by the Institute for Advanced Studies 1961. The typescript *'Guide to the county Limerick estate records'* is also available in the reading room of the NLI and NAI.
The largest single collection of documents relating to estates is the records of the Encumbered Estates Courts, established in the mid 19th century to administer the public sale of bankrupt estates. In the aftermath of the great famine many landlords became bankrupt and their estates were sold through special court sittings. Both NAI and NLI have good collections of this source.

Specific sources for Limerick Estate records include:

Ballingarry, Granagh and Clouncagh Archival Records 1800-1900 by Christy Kerins (Dublin 2000) lists rentals for the Ballingarry area.
Survey of Leaseholders on the Desmond Estates of West Limerick for 1586. NAI M. 5037; LDS film 0258793-0258850.
'Bishop Webb's rental of the lands of the Diocese of Limerick' N.Mun.Arch.Soc. Jnl. 1916, 4 (1) p. 25-47
Rental of the Courtenay/ Devon estate 1764-1766 and a rental for 1828 held by Limerick Archives
Estate Records of the Irish Famine. Andres Eiriksson & Cormac O'Grada. Irish Famine Network, TCD 1995. (lists estate records for Limerick, giving location, types of record, and reference).

Rental of the estate of Lord Emly (William Monsell) 1888-1894 on LDS film.
This is a microfilm of the ms. held at Glenstal Abbey, Murroe, Co. Limerick.
Monteagle estate rentals, 1830-1850 Held at Limerick Archives.
These papers contain numerous estate ledgers which list tenants as well as rent
rolls.

There are also extensive papers relating to specific Limerick families that
are worth checking, as they sometimes include references to tenants. The
Kenmare estates in Limerick are referred to in *The Kenmare Manuscripts*
edited by Edward McLysaght Dublin, IMC 1942. The book includes numerous
references to the Hospital locality and there are tithe listings as far back as
1722. There are also ledgers relating to the Kenmare estates in Limerick and
Kerry on LDS film (check the LDS catalogue on the internet for details).
The Monteagle Papers (1834-1850) are available in Limerick Archives, they
can also be checked for you by the staff of Limerick Ancestry. These estate
papers are also held in the NLI and relate to the Spring and Rice families and
their property in Counties Limerick and Kerry up to 1925. They include a
rental book for the estate of Stephen Edward Rice 1788-1810 and a rental for
Mount Trenchard   from 1747.

THE LANDOWNERS OF IRELAND.			351
Name, Titles, and Addresses.	County.	Acreage.	Valuation. £
O'GRADY, EDWARD STAMER, M.B., C.H. M.F.; Abbeyfeale ; 105 Stephen's Green, South, Dublin.	Limerick -	1438	·519
O'GRADY, GEORGE FRANCIS. Educated at Trin. Coll., Dublin ; late Capt. 2nd. Queen's Royal and 56th Regts.; Tavrane, Ballyhaunis, co. Mayo ; Junior United Service Club, s.w.; United Service Club, Dublin.	Galway - Mayo - Roscommon	·654 1342 1099 3095	275 555 310 114ᴜ
O'GRADY, GILBERT, late Lieut. 78th Highlanders,—Landscape, Clonlara, co, Clare.	Clare - Limerick '-	63 1488 1551	94 769 863
O'GRADY, Hon. CECILIA, Rochbarton, Bruff.	Limerick -	4977	4070
O'GRADY, Hon. Mrs. JANE STEWART, Plattenstown, Arklow, co Wicklow	Wexford -	·730	508

A page from *The Landowners of Ireland* by U.H. De Burgh(1878).

Chapter 4   Census and Census Substitutes

Census returns are a basic information source for the researcher. The first national census was taken in 1821, and was repeated every ten years. However, the individual household returns are available only for 1901 and 1911. Returns from 1926 and later have not yet been made public. Returns for earlier years were destroyed for various reasons some to protect confidentiality; others to make paper during World War I and the remainder in the Public Records Office (now the NAI) fire in 1922. Fragments of some of the returns for the years 1821, 1831,1841 and 1851 have survived, (see census substitutes for Kifinane below). The 1901 and 1911 censuses are the earliest complete returns for the whole country including County Limerick. They are therefore a very valuable source of information.

A census household return gives information on the age, family relationship, occupation, literacy, place of birth and marital status of each household occupant. The 1911 returns note the number of children born to each couple, how long they were married and the number living at the time of the census. Both censuses also provide a description of the dwelling place of each household. This can help locate your ancestors in a socio-economic group.

To find an ancestor you need to know their address at the time. In rural areas you will need a townland, and in urban areas a street address. Other sources may have to be used by the researcher to establish an address. Birth, baptism, or marriage records generally provide this information. Street directories, headstone inscriptions or an old family bible can sometimes provide a family address at a particular time.

In 1908 old age pensions were introduced for persons who could prove that they were over the age of 70. However, civil registration only began in 1864 so birth certificates were not available as a proof of age. Many people therefore used the censuses to prove their age, and therefore eligibility for a pension. They applied to the government for a certificate showing that they were listed in the 1841 and/or 1851 census. The Public Records Office (NAI) verified the claims by issuing a 'Green form' to the applicant. Some of these forms have survived and are in the National Archives. There is a census search form index for Co. Limerick. It is arranged by barony, civil parish and townland. However, the numbers of entries amount to less than 4,000. This is because baptism registers were the first source appealed to, so that names in the 'green forms' are often from parishes which did not have records that were old enough.

The 1901 and 1911 censuses are available at the Limerick city and county libraries and in Limerick Ancestry. A complete set of returns for the 1901 and 1911 census are also held in the NAI. Another miscellaneous source for the twentieth century are the ms. maps of the lands of Palles, Co. Limerick the estate of the governors of Erasmus Smiths' schools with names of tenants by Sherrard Brassington and Greene 1918 held by the NLI.

The following list gives other census substitutes one can search in **nineteenth century** records.

1803-1810: The Kane Papers - Captain Kane's record book of Co. Limerick Regiment militia. Limerick City Archives.

1813: "The Chief Inhabitants of the Parishes of St. Mary's and St. John's Limerick in 1813" by Rosemary ffolliott *Ir.Anc.* 1985, 17 (2) p. 75-77

1814-1823: List of those convicted during the period 1814-1823. Parliamentary Papers, 1824 vol. 22.

1816-1828: List of Freeholders for the County of Limerick GO ms.623; LDS film 1000224

1816: 'Voters in the Limerick City Election of 1817.' by Rosemary ffolliott *Ir. Anc.* 1985, 17 (1) p. 49-57 and NLI IR324LI

1819-1941: 'Certain statistics from the united parishes of Knockainey and Patrickswell for the years 1819- 1941' by Rev. C. Lee in JCHAS 47 p. 1-3

1820: Two registers of voters or canvassers notebooks c.1820 NLI ms.14, 118-9

1821: 'Fragments of Census Returns for Kilfinane District' by Mainchin Seoighe in NMAJ 1975, 17, p. 83-90. Contains notes from the 1821 census relating to the townlands of Ballyshonekin (Effin parish), Ballyrigan, Kilfinnane, Ballyorgan (Kilflyn parish), Mortelstown and Sunville (Particles parish) all in Co.Limerick. Copies of census returns relating to the White family of Co.Limerick NAI ms. 5246 (1-2).

1823: The Limerick city assizes and quarter sessions. These people were committed for trial under the Insurrection Act of 1823-24.

1823-1838: Tithe Applotment Survey (see previous chapter) NLI ms.6922

1829: Limerick's Freeholders, with Addresses and Occupations. GO M62

1829: Limerick Game Licenses recorded those licensed to shoot and hunt game. The lists were printed in the Limerick Chronicle and those for the period 1809-1821 can be accessed at *http://home.att.net/~labaths/game.htm* Readers can also check ffolliott's article 'Game licences in county Limerick 1802-1821' *Ir. Anc.* 1984, 16 (2) p. 98-106

1834: "The population of a rural pre-famine parish – Templebredin, Co. Limerick and Tipperary in 1834' by Fergus O'Ferrall in NMAJ 1975 17 p. 91-101

1835-1839: Lists of residents of Limerick in Waterworks accounts. NLI Pos.3451. Survey of Moher and Furkeal in the parish of Abington, barony of Owneybeg (estate of Lord Cloncurry) with names of tenants NAI. ms.9053

1837: List of applicants who served notice on the clerks of the peace for the county of the city of Limerick of their intention to register as voters April 1837. [from The Limerick Chronicle newspaper March 1837] Held in Limerick City library.

1840: List of Freeholders in the Barony of Coshlea. NLI ms.9452

1841: 'Emigration to North America from the port of Limerick 1841' by Michael Hewson NMAJ 1981 23 p. 67-76. Copies of census returns relating to the Doody family of Limerick City NAI ms.5248 (1 3); Copies of census returns relating to the Harnett family NAI ms.5248 (19); Copies of census returns relating to the Elmes family of Limerick city ms. M 5248 (23).

1843: Voters List. NAI 1843/66.

1846: Survey of Households in Connection with Famine Relief. NLI ms.582 (Loughill, Foynes and Shanagolden area).

1848: Petitioners for William Smith O'Brien. Names of male petitioners in Abbeyfeale and Limerick City. NAI 1848/180. These names are now available on CD-ROM published by Eneclann Ltd. (*www.eneclann.ie*)
J.S. Armstrong's, *A report of trials under a special commission for the county of Limerick held at Limerick January 1848* deals with some twenty trials arising from an outbreak of a series of violent crimes in the county. 'List of men who took part in the Fenian uprising in Ardagh, Co. Limerick' by Edward Keane is in NMAJ 1967 10 (1) p. 79-82. Also on the Magner clan site at www.magner.org/research/fenian.htm

1849: The NLI holds ms. 2024 a list of law actions in Limerick city and county courts with names of parties and attorneys etc. compiled by William D'Alton 1849-51.

1850: *The Millers and Mills of Ireland of about 1850* by William Hogg pub. Dublin, Wm. Hogg, 1998. Includes name of miller and addresses. Limerick millers are on p. 85-92.

1850-1852: Griffiths Valuation (see previous chapter, *see also* p.113)

1851: Kilfinane-see 1821 re: census fragments. The NAI has ms.7156; extract from census of 1851 re: family of Conners, Toomdeely South, Barony of Connello Lower, Co.Limerick; Copies of census returns relating to the Scanlon family NAI ms.5249 (69); Copies of census returns relating to the Wallace family of Limerick city NAI ms. 5247 (77).

1867: 'List of Active Fenians in Co. Limerick' by Edward Keane NMAJ 1967 10 (2) p. 169-172. Also in this same volume is an article called 'Mourning the martyrs – a study of a demonstration in Limerick city 8/12/67' by Brendan Mac Giolla Choille. This gives a return of persons in the procession as identified by the police. Occupations and place of residence are also given - see NMAJ 1967 10 (2) p. 173-197

1867-1945: Robert Herbert's article 'The antiquaries of the corporation of Limerick' in NMAJ 1945 4 (3) p. 85-127 lists the freemen, mayors and sheriffs for the city of Limerick for this period.

1901: Government Census (see start of chapter, *see also* p.113).

1911: Government Census (see start of chapter, *see also* p.113).

Eighteenth century records include the following:

1700s: 'Limerick men in the Hotel Royal des Invalides', Paris by Eoghan O'hAnnrachain A list of men who served abroad following the defeat of King James's forces in Ireland. an appendix to the article gives their names, in some cases their place of origin in Limerick, regiment, wounds, profession and marital status, NMAJ (42) p.35-68.

1715-1794: Freemen of the City of Limerick. PRO(London); LDS film 477000

1746-1836: Index to the Freemen of Limerick in 'The Antiquaries of the Corporation of Limerick', NMAJ 1945 4 (3) p. 85 -127.

1761: Militia List. Counties Limerick etc. GO ms.680; Names and addresses of freeholders voting in a parliamentary election. NLI ms.16093

1766: Householders of Parishes of Abington, Ardcanny, Cahircomey,

CENSUS OF IRELAND, 1901.

FORM A.

No. on Form B.

(Two Examples of the mode of filling up this Table are given on the other side.)

RETURN of the MEMBERS of this FAMILY and their VISITORS, BOARDERS, SERVANTS, &c. who slept or abode in this House on the night of SUNDAY, the 31st of MARCH 1901.

No.	NAME and SURNAME	RELATION to Head of Family	RELIGIOUS PROFESSION	EDUCATION	AGE (Years)	AGE (Months)	SEX	RANK, PROFESSION, OR OCCUPATION	MARRIAGE	WHERE BORN	IRISH LANGUAGE	If Deaf and Dumb &c.
1	Denis Ryan	Head of Family	Roman catholic	Read and write	60	—	M	Farmer	Married	County of Limerick		
2	Johanna Ryan	Wife	Roman catholic	Read & write	54	—	F		Married	County Limerick		
3	John Ryan	Son	Roman catholic	Read & write	30	—	M	Farmer son	Not married	County Limerick		
4	Roger Ryan	Son	Roman catholic	Read & write	24	—	M	Farmer son	Not married	County Limerick		
5	Ellay Ryan	Daughter	Roman catholic	Read & write	20	—	F	Farmer daughter	Not married	County Limerick		
6	Catherine Ryan	Daughter	Roman catholic	Read & write	18	—	F	Farmer daughter	Not married	County Limerick		
7	Johanna Ryan	Daughter	Roman catholic	Read & write	12	—	F	Farmer daughter	Not married	County Limerick		

I hereby certify, as required by the Act 63 Vic, cap. 6, s. 6 (1), that the foregoing Return is correct, according to the best of my knowledge and belief.

(Signature of Enumerator.)

I believe the foregoing to be a true Return.

Denis Ryan *(Signature of Head of Family)*

A typical return from the 1901 Census of Ireland

Cahirelly, Carrigparson, Clonkeen, Kilkellane and Tuogh. NAI; Parliamentary Papers 681/684. Protestant householders of parishes of Clonagh, Croagh, Dondaniel, Kilscannel, Nantinan and Rathkeale. GO 537; RCBL ms.37; LDS film 258517; also transcribed in *Ir.Anc.*1977 9 (2) p. 77-78.
List of Protestants and Papists in Limerick Diocese. GO 540; LDS film 100212
1767: 'Some notes on Parliament and its Limerick members' by Cliodna Snoddy in NMAJ 1965 10 (4) p.165-181.

1776: Names of the owners of freeholds entitled to vote. NAI mf. 1321-22

1783: *A list of freeholders who voted at the election for Knights of the Shire at St. Francis's abbey on 25 Aug. 1783 and continued by adjournments to the 6 September following.* Printed by Andrew Watson a Limerick printer. Held in NLI.

1793: 'Two lists of persons resident in the vicinity of Newcastle in 1793 and 1821' by Rosemary ffolliott. *Ir. Anc.* 1984 16 (1) p. 40-44

1796: Flax Grower List of 1796. This gives the full name and civil parish of people growing flax, NLI ir 677 L3. This list is available on CD-ROM by Family Tree Makers Family Archives. The NAI also has a microfiche index.

1798: "List of Rebel Prisoners in Limerick Gaol' by Edward Keane.
NMAJ 1967 10 (1) p. 79-82

1799: 'Gentlemen of the Counties Clare and Limerick who were in favour of the Union in 1799' transcribed by Rosemary ffolliott in *Ir. Anc.* 1982 14 (1) p. 32-35 and OLJ no.37 Summer 2001.

In the **seventeenth century** the two principal sources are the *Civil Survey of 1654-56* (see previous chapter) and the *1659 "Census" of Ireland* edited by Pender (see opposite). These are available in hardcopy in the both the National Library of Ireland and many other libraries. They are also available from the LDS (civil survey film no.973122 and census film no. 924648). The NLI holds the *'Book of Survey and Distribution'* compiled c.1703, which lists proprietors of land in 1641 and grantees of land distributed in 1666-68, with acreage. There is a rental of lands in Limerick city and county for 1660 in the NLI ms.9091. Also in 1673 there is a description of part of Limerick city (estates of the earls of Roscommon and Orrery) with occupier's names and valuations. This is held in the NLI pos. 7922.

There is a paucity of records extant for the **sixteenth century**. You can however check a List of Freeholders and Gentlemen in Co.Limerick in 1570

NLI P1700 also in J. H. Pierse's article NMAJ 1964 9 (3) p. 108-112. A Calendar of portion of the Desmond Survey NAI ms.5038 and A Calendar by M.J McEnery of Peyton's survey of 1586 NAI ms.5039;2759.

Finally one can look in *The Fiants of the Tudor Sovereigns*. This worthy publication covers the fiants or warrants directed to the Irish chancery ordering the issue of letters patent. The fiants are a rich genealogical source and cover the periods of the reigns of Henry V111, Edmund V1, Philip, Mary and Elizabeth I. They record an estimated 120,000 names of individuals and give the historical form of Irish personal names, surnames and placenames. This publication has been published by De Burca Antiquarian Books of Blackrock,Co. Dublin.

274   CENSUS OF IRELAND, 1659

(folio 12).   **CLANWILLIAM BARRONY.**

Parrishes	Townelands	Number of People	Tituladoes Names	Eng	Irish
	Robertstowne	46			46
	Ballinroan	04			04
	Rochtowne	17			17
	Ballinloghane	37			37
	Fryarstowne	08			08
	Williamstowne	17	Edward Andrewes gent	04	13
	BallyMcGnard	83	Captn Faithfull Chapman	03	80
	Whytstowne	68	James Casy gent		68
	Kilcooline	36	Wm Cobb & Thymotie Dickson gent	07	29
	Ballymakree	13			13
	Luddenbeg	31	Edmond Bourke & Mortagh Ó Beara gent		31
	Sthrahane	41	John Hale & Wm Clearke gents	06	35
	Knockatanacushland	47	John Friend Esq & Edward Willy gents	13	34
	Cahercourceely	38	Donogh Ó Hea gent	06	32
	Inchy Lawrence	07			07
	Greenarrebegg	44			44
	Knock Ineagh	24	John Loftus gent	04	20
(folio 13).	Boherskeaghaganiffe	17	Richard Willy & Nathalian Watts gents	06	11
	Cloghnadromon	16		02	14
	Kishy Quirke	14	John Syms gent	05	09
	Lismollane	22	Thomas Burton gent	04	18
	Caherkinlish	66	Stephen Towes gent	03	63
	Boskill and Temple Michell	39	Humphrey Curteois & Edmond Curteois gent	07	32
	Castlevorkine	41	Edward Allen gent	02	39
	Both Greenanes	20		—	20
	Ballyvorneene	39	Wm Ingram gent	01	38
	Killenure and Gortinskeagh	18	Wm Chapman gent	02	16
	Graingerbegg	17	John Cooke gent	02	15

A page from *Pender's Census of Ireland, 1659*.

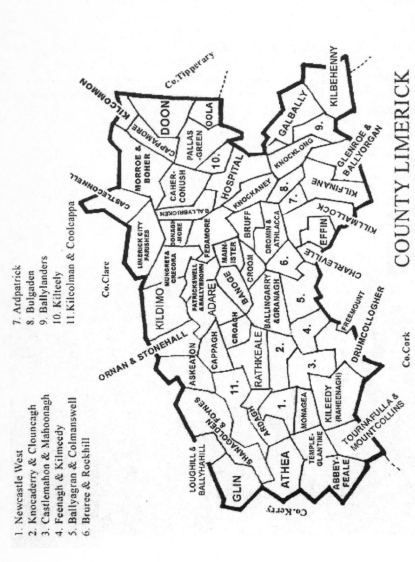

1. Newcastle West
2. Knocaderry & Clouncagh
3. Castlemahon & Mahoonagh
4. Feenagh & Kilmeedy
5. Ballyagran & Colmanswell
6. Bruree & Rockhill
7. Ardpatrick
8. Bulgaden
9. Ballylanders
10. Kilteely
11. Kilcolman & Coolcappa

Roman Catholic Parishes from *The Limerick Rural Survey 1958-64*, edited by Jeremiah Nowlan (Muintir na Tíre, 1964).

Chapter 5 Church Records

Church records are the most important source of genealogical information prior to 1864 when civil registration of births, marriages and deaths began. For the period before 1864 parish registers of baptisms, marriages and burials provide us with the only source of such information. To effectively use church records you must obviously know your ancestor's religion, and some idea of the place of baptism, marriage or burial. Limerick people are predominantly either Catholic or Church or Ireland, but there are also congregations of Presbyterians (see 5.3), Methodists (5.4), Palatines (5.5), Jews (5.6) and Quakers (5.7).

5.1   Roman Catholic Records

When seeking Roman Catholic records you need to bear in mind that this church existed under severe restrictions from the late 17th century up to the late 18th century. Though the Catholic church represented about eighty percent of the population it was repressed very severely. The Penal Laws, passed in the first years of the 18th century, proscribed many elements of the Catholic church's infrastructure and activities, and also banned Catholics from many occupations, public positions and property ownership. These repressive measures directly and indirectly affected the keeping of records. Although the more repressive measures were relaxed during the late 18th century, it was not until after the Catholic Emancipation Act of 1829 that full rights were restored to Catholics.

The Roman Catholic parish registers are almost all held locally, but they are also almost all held on on microfilms in the National Library and LDS libraries. These records are not standardized and vary in quality from register to register. The most useful of baptismal records give the name of the child, the name and address of the father, maiden name of the mother, names of sponsors and the dates.   Marriage entries at best give the date of the marriage and the names of the bride, groom and the witnesses. The way in which the information was recorded also varies. Latin is used in some registers e.g. 'baptizatus' for baptised, 'matrimonium' or married; 'sepultus' or buried. The quality of the registers also varies; in some cases the poor handwriting makes deciphering the records extremely difficult.

The National library has microfilm copies of all registers up to 1880. Note that for some records you may need the permission of the bishop. This is the case with the registers of the dioceses of Cashel and Emly which cover some 25%

of the county. It is also necessary to get the approval of the bishop of Kerry for parishes in this diocese (see chapter 15).

The National Library has an excellent guide to getting started in Catholic church records, it is available on the internet at *www.nli.ie* There is also a list of Roman Catholic parish records at *www.rootsweb.com/~fianna/county/ limerick/limrc.html*

If you are uncertain which diocese covers the area of interest to you, you should consult the *Irish Catholic Directory* for a recent year. This is available in most Irish libraries. This lists the parishes and the dioceses of Limerick. Remember when searching to allow for variations in surname spelling e.g. Connor, Connors, O'Connor. As the Catholic registers are not state records they are still in local custody. In order to see them you should get in touch with the local parish priest in your area of interest. Below is a list of the Roman Catholic parishes. It provides the starting date of the records held by the parishes. It also indicates 'Index: LA' for those records which are indexed by Limerick Ancestry up to 1900 and 'THU' for those held by Thurles Heritage Unit up to 1899. If you want to contact a particular parish you will find the name and address of the relevant parish priest in the *Irish Catholic Directory*. There is also an internet site at www. local.ie/general/genealogy/ roman_catholic_registers. However, you should be aware that many priests may not answer such letters as they have made their records available both for microfilming and for indexing by heritage centres. The Limerick Diocese also has an excellent website *www.limerickdiocese.org* which gives extensive information on many parishes, graveyards and townlands.

Finally note that you can order microfilms of Limerick registers at your local LDS Family History Centre. The Limerick centre has only recently opened and is giving a limited service by appointment only. Limerick Ancestry has all of Limerick on computer but charges a research fee (see both at chapter 13).

Roman Catholic Parishes of Limerick:

Abbeyfeale
Diocese:LK
Baptisms:1829
Marriages:1856
Index: LA.

Ardagh
Diocese:LK
Baptisms:1845
Marriages:1841
Index: LA.

Adare
Diocese:LK
Baptisms:1832
Marriages:1832
Index: LA.

Ardpatrick
Diocese:LK
Baptisms:1861
Marriages:1861
Index: LA.

Askeaton
Diocese:LK
Baptisms:1829
Marriages:1829
Index: LA.

Athea
Diocese:LK
Baptisms:1830
Marriages:1827

Ballingarry
Diocese:LK
Baptisms:1825
Marriages:1825
Index: LA.

Ballyagran & Colemanswell
Diocese:LK
Baptisms:1841
Marriages:1841
Index: LA.

Ballybricken & Bohermore
Diocese:EM
Baptisms:1800
Marriages:1805
Index: LA.

Ballylanders
Diocese:EM
Baptisms:1849
Marriages:1857
Index: LA & THU

Bruff
Diocese:LK
Baptisms:1781
Marriages:1781
Index: LA.

Bulgaden & Ballinvana
Diocese:LK
Baptisms:1812

Marriages:1812
Index: LA.

Caherconlish
Diocese:EM
Baptisms:1841
Marriages:1841
Index: LA & THU.

Cappagh
Diocese:LK
Baptisms:1841
Marriages:1841
Index: LA.

Cappamore
Diocese:EM
Baptisms:1845
Marriages:1843
Index: LA. & THU.

Castleconnell Previous part of
Kilcornan
Diocese:KL
Baptisms:1850
Marriages:1863
Index: LA.

Croagh & Kilfinny
Diocese:LK
Baptisms:1836
Marriages:1844
Index: LA.

Croom
Diocese:LK
Baptisms:1828
Marriages:1770
Notes:Civil parishes of Anhid &
Dysert. Also deaths from 1770. LA to
1900

Donaghmore & Knockea
Diocese:LK

Baptisms:1830
Marriages:1827
Index: LA.

Doon & Castletown also part
Cappamore
Diocese:EM
Baptisms:1824
Marriages:1839
Index: LA & THU.

Dromin & Athlacca
Diocese:LK
Baptisms:1817
Marriages:1817
Index: LA.

Dromcollogher & Broadford
Diocese:LK
Baptisms:1830
Marriages:1830
Index: LA.

Effin & Garrenderk
Diocese:LK
Baptisms:1843
Marriages:1843
Index: LA.

Fedamore
Diocese:LK
Baptisms:1806
Marriages:1806

Feenagh & Kilmeedy
Diocese:LK
Baptisms:1833
Marriages:1854
Index: LA.

Galbally
Diocese:EM
Baptisms:1810
Marriages:1809
Index: LA.

Glenroe & Ballyorgan
Diocese:LK
Baptisms:1853
Marriages:1853
Index: LA.

Glin
Diocese:LK
Baptisms:1851
Marriages:1851
Index: LA.

Hospital & Herbertstown
Diocese:EM
Baptisms:1810
Marriages:1812
Index: THU.

Kilbehenny
Diocese:EM
Baptisms:1824
Marriages:1825
Index: LA & THU.

Kilcoleman & Coolcappa
Diocese:LK
Baptisms:1827
Marriages:1828

Kilcornan
Diocese:LK
Baptisms:1825
Marriages:1825
Index: LA.

Kildimo & Chapelrussel
Diocese:LK
Baptisms:1831
Marriages:1831
Index: LA.

Kilfinane
Diocese:LK
Baptisms:1832
Marriages:1832

Index: LA.

Kilmallock
Diocese:LK
Baptisms:1837
Marriages:1837
Index: LA.

Kilteely & Dromkeen
Diocese:EM
Baptisms:1815
Marriages:1832
Index: LA & THU.

Knockaney & Patrickswell
Diocese:EM
Baptisms:1808
Marriages:1808
Deaths: 1819.
Index: LA & THU.

Knockaderry & Cloncagh
Diocese:LK
Baptisms:1838
Marriages:1838
Index: LA.

Knocklong & Glenbrohane
Diocese:EM
Baptisms:1809
Marriages:1809
Index: LA & THU.

St. John's
Diocese:LK
Baptisms:1788
Marriages:1821
Index: LA.

St. Mary's
Diocese:LK
Baptisms:1745
Marriages:1745
Index: LA.

St. Michael's
Diocese:LK
Baptisms:1776
Marriages:1772
Index: LA.

St. Munchin's
Diocese:LK
Baptisms:1764
Marriages:1764

St. Patrick's
Diocese:LK
Baptisms:1805
Marriages:1806
Index: LA.

Loughill (previously part of Glin)
& Ballyhahill (previously part of
Shanagolden)
Diocese:LK
Baptisms:1855
Marriages:1855
Index: LA.

Mahoonagh
Diocese:LK
Baptisms:1812
Marriages:1810
Index: LA.

Manister
Diocese:LK
Baptisms:1826
Marriages:1826
Index: LA.

Monagea
Diocese:LK
Baptisms:1776
Marriages:1777
Index: LA.

Mungret & Crecora
Diocese:LK
Baptisms:1844
Marriages:1844
Index: LA.

Murroe & Boher
Diocese:EM
Baptisms:1814
Marriages:1815
Index: LA & THU.

Newcastlewest
Diocese:LK
Baptisms:1815
Marriages:1815
Index: LA.

Oola & Sologhead
Diocese:EM
Baptisms:1809
Marriages:1810
Index: LA & THU.

Pallasgrean
Diocese:EM
Baptisms:1811
Marriages:1811
Index: THU.

Patrickswell
Diocese:LK
Baptisms:1801
Marriages:1802

Rathkeale
Diocese:LK
Baptisms:1811
Marriages:1811
Index: LA.

Rockhill & Bruree
Diocese:LK
Baptisms:1842
Marriages:1861
Index: LA.

Shanagolden & Foynes
Diocese:LK
Baptisms:1824
Marriages:1824

Templeglantine (previous part of Monagea)
Diocese:LK
Baptisms:1864
Marriages:1865
Index: LA.

Tournafulla/Mountcollins
Diocese:LK
Baptisms:1840
Marriages:1840
Index: LA.

5.2 Church of Ireland Records

The boundaries of Church of Ireland parishes are usually the same as civil parishes. Baptismal records provide information on the name of the child, the father's name, the mother's first name and the name of the clergyman. Marriage records usually provide the names of the parties marrying and the name of the clergyman. From 1845 all non-Catholic marriages were registered by the state and the marriage records became more detailed. They record all the information contained in state records including occupation, addresses and father's names. These records are stored in the GRO (see chapter 6).

When the Church of Ireland was disestablished in 1869 most of its records to that date became public records. Legislation required that the Church's baptismal and burial records up to 1870 and marriages up to 1845 be deposited in the Public Record Office (now the NAI). This was later amended to allow the Church of Ireland to retain copies of registers locally. In 1922 the fire at the PRO destroyed the stored registers, which made up approximately 33% of all registers. However copies of the post 1844 marriage registers survived because these were stored in the General Register Office where they are still available and fully indexed.

Church of Ireland parish records also include vestry books. These contain the minutes of the vestry meetings of the local parish. They can give detailed information about parishioners. They record such details as local tax collections, the local constabulary, arrangement for the care of orphans, and other duties and activities of the church.

The RCBL holds vestry books for Abington (EM) 1811-1871, Ballinlanders (EM) 1862-1873 and Cappamore (EM) 1858-1893, four volumes of vestry books for Duntryleague 1766-1830 and Sunday School Attendance Books for Castleconnell (KL) 1890-1911. The NLI has a vestry book for Rathkeale,1748-79 and the parish of St. Peter and Paul Kilmallock, 1775-1815.
The NAI has a vestry book for Ballingarry while Glin vestry books are held at the University of Limerick.

The LDS library has an index to the marriages in county Limerick before 1st April 1845. The call number for this film is 941.94K22L. The registers indexed include Abington, Adare, Aney, Ardcanny and others. Check the LDS catalog on the web for a full listing – search using 'Limerick' as a keyword.
Another useful source is ms.2541in the NAI, a petition of distressed Protestants of Connello and Kenry baronies for the late 17th. century.

Below is a list of the Church of Ireland parish records it also indicates 'Index: LA' for those records indexed by Limerick Ancestry up to 1980. For the addresses of local clergymen, you can check the current *Church of Ireland Directory*. Remember that this directory is organised by Diocese rather than county. You may have to get permission from the local clergy to be allowed access records in the NAI. For a more complete account of these records take a look at Raymond Refausse's article 'Records of the Church of Ireland' in *Irish Church Records*, edited by James G, Ryan (Flyleaf Press, Dublin 2001). The LDS have microfilms of many Church of Ireland records, those for Limerick are also listed below:

Church of Ireland Parishes of Limerick:

Abington:
Baptisms 1811
Marriages 1813
Burials 1810
Location LC, NAI

Adare:
Baptisms 1826
Marriages 1826
Burials 1826
Location NLI, LDS film 874437
　　　　　Index: LA.

Aney:
Baptisms 1760
Marriages 1761
Burials 1759
Location *J. Ir. Mem Assoc.* 12

Ardcanny and **Chapelrussel:**
Baptisms 1802
Marriages 1802
Burials 1805
Location LC, NLI, NAI,
　　　　　LDS film 928607
　　　　　Index: LA.

Askeaton:
Baptisms 1877
Marriages 1845
Burials 1877
Location LC, Index: LA

Ballingarry:
Baptisms 1785
Marriages 1785
Burials 1785
Location GO 701, LDS film
　　　　　257807, film 101780
　　　　　Index: LA.

Ballinlanders:
Marriages 1852-1877
Location RCBL

Bruff:
Baptisms 1859
Marriages 1845
Burials 1859
Location LC, NAI, Index: LA.

Caherconlish:
Baptisms 1888
Marriages 1845
Burials 1890
Location LC, Index: LA.

Cahernarry:(See also
St.Mary's)
Baptisms 1855
Marriages 1847
Burials 1877
Location LC, NAI, Index: LA.

Cappamore & Tuogh:
Baptisms 1859
Marriages 1845
Burials 1859
Location LC, Index: LA.

Corcomohide:
Baptisms 1805
Marriages 1805
Burials 1805
Location LC, NAI

Croom:
Baptisms 1877
Marriages 1848
Burials 1880
Location LC, Index: LA.

Doon:
Baptisms	1804
Marriages	1812
Burials	1812
Location	LC, NAI, LDS film 990092

Fedamore:
Baptisms	1840
Marriages	1845
Location	LC, NAI, Index: LA.

Kilcornan:
Baptisms	1892
Marriages	1845
Burials	1893
Location	LC, Index: LA.

Kildimo:
Baptisms	1809
Marriages	1809
Burials	1809
Location	LC

Kilfergus & Kilmoylan:
Baptisms	1812
Marriages	1815
Burials	1836
Location	LC, NAI, Index: LA.

Kilfinane:
Baptisms	1804
Marriages	1804
Burials	1798
Location	LC, NAI, LDS film 897422 Index: LA.

Kilflyn:
Baptisms	1813
Marriages	1813
Burials	1813
Location	LC, Index: LA.

Kilkeedy:
Baptisms	1802
Marriages	1802
Burials	1799
Location	LC, Index: LA.

Killaliathan:
Baptisms	1879
Marriages	1851
Burials	1883
Location	LC, Index: LA.

Killeedy:
Baptisms	1879
Marriages	1846
Location	LC, Index: LA.

Kilmallock:
Baptisms	1883
Marriages	1846
Burials	1883
Location	LC, Index: LA.

Kilmeedy:
Baptisms	1805
Marriages	1805
Burials	1805
Location	LC, NAI, LDS film 897422 Index: LA.

Kilpeacon: (See also Rathkeale)
Baptisms	1892
Marriages	1845
Burials	1895
Location	LC, Index: LA.

Kilscannell:
Baptisms	1824
Marriages	1825
Burials	1860
Location	LC, NAI, Index: LA.

Knockainy:
Baptisms   1883
Marriages   1845
Burials   1883
Location   LC, Index: LA.

Limerick City
Garrison:
Baptisms   1858
Burials   1865
Location   LC, NAI

Lk.City- St. John's:
Baptisms   1697
Marriages   1697
Burials   1697
Location   LC, NAI, LDS film
            874438 Index: LA.

Lk. City- St. Laurence:
Baptisms   1863
Burials   1697
Location   LC

Lk. City- St. Mary's:
Baptisms   1726
Marriages   1726
Burials   1726
Location   LC, NAI, LDS film
            897365 Index: LA.

Lk. City- St. Michael's:
Baptisms   1803
Marriages   1799
Burials   1803
Location   LC, NAI, LDS film
            897422 Index: LA.

Lk. City- St. Munchin:
Baptisms   1700
Marriages   1700
Burials   1700
Location   LC, LDS film 897365
            Index: LA.

Loughill:
Marriages   1846
Burials   1883
Location   LC, Index: LA.

Mahoonagh:
Baptisms   1861
Location   LC, NAI

Mungret:
Baptisms   1852
Marriages   1845
Burials   1843
Location   LC, NAI, Index: LA.

Nantinan:
Baptisms   1877
Marriages   1845
Burials   1848
Location   LC, Index: LA.

Newcastle:
Baptisms   1842
Marriages   1845
Burials   1848
Location   LC, NAI, Index: LA.

Particles:
Baptisms   1841
Marriages   1800
Burials   1812
Location   LC, NAI, Index: LA.

Rathkeale:
Baptisms   1742
Marriages   1742
Burials   1742
Location   LC, NAI, LDS film
            897365

Rathronan and
Ardagh:
Baptisms   1720
Marriages   1722
Burials   1722
Location   LC, NAI

Shanagolden:

Baptisms	1879
Marriages	1847
Burials	1881
Location	LC, Index: LA.

Stradbally:

Baptisms	1792
Marriages	1787
Burials	1789
Location	LC, NAI, Index: LA.

Michael Leader, a Vice-President of the Irish Genealogical Research Society (London), died in 1998 leaving a large collection of transcribed Church of Ireland parish registers to this society. The collection mainly covers County Cork but occasionally covers other counties especially when a diocesan boundary extended into another county. They were transcribed between the 1950's and the 1990's.

The transcriptions were made from either the original parish registers or from transcripts held by the Public Records Office in Dublin (now the NAI). Much of Leader's early work was done in partnership with Rosemary ffolliot who also transcribed many registers. All the Limerick registers listed below were transcribed by ffolliot and are part of the Michael Leader collection. They are also all from the diocese of Limerick. For a full description of the Leader collection see Mary Casteleyn's article in the *Ir. Gen.* 1999, 10, 2 p. 173-201 from which the following list is taken.

Leader Collection:

Adare

baptisms 1826-1866
marriages 1826-1844
burials 1825-1878

Ardcanny
baptisms 1802-1927
marriages 1802-1844
burials (and baptisms) 1805-1894

Ballingarry
Taken from Betham's copy
(ref.PROI 1A.44.25)
baptisms 1698-1735,1840-1908
marriages 1698-1733/4, 1840-66,
1845-1906
burials (and marriage) 1698-1734/5,
1785/1790, 1785-1804, 1840-1927
marriages and burials 1802-1840

confirmations (and conversions from Popery) 1845,1850,1855

Corcomohide (see also **Kilmeedy**)
marriages 1845-1882

Croagh
marriages 1850-1868

Kilfinane
baptisms 1804-1807, 1844-1865
marriages 1804-1845
burials 1798-1849

Killaliathan
baptisms 1879-1916 (in the same volume as Killeedy)

marriages 1851-1908
burials 1883-1919

Killeedy
baptisms 1879-1885
marriages 1847-1892

Kilmeedy (see also **Corcomohide**)
combined register 1805-1895, index

Kilscannel
baptisms 1824-1895
marriages 1825-59, 1845-1886
burials 18650-1887
index
list of surnames used as Christian
names

Mahoonagh
burials 1861-64

Nantenan
births 1783-1833 (source *Ir. Anc.*14, 1
p. 22-24)
baptisms 1877-1904
marriages 1784-1821(source *Ir.Anc.*as
above)
marriages 1845-1900
burials 1783-1820 (source *Ir.Anc.*as
above.)
burials 1878-1924

Newcastle
baptisms 1848-1916
marriages 1845-1888
burials 1848-1912

Rathkeale
Renounciations of Romish religion
1744-55
baptisms 1742-1899
marriages 1743/4-1845, 1845-1901
burials 1741905
St. John's
christenings 1697-1817, 1818-1836
marriages 1697-1837
burials 1697-1746, 1746-1837

St. Mary's Cathedral
baptisms 1726-96
weddings 1726-1801
burials 1726-1799
purifications 1775
register 1800-1826

St. Michael's
christenings 1803-1809
weddings 1799-1810,1827-44
baptisms 1825-1844
burials 1827-1844
combined register 1809-1834

St. Munchin's
combined register 1734-1768,1797-
1808
baptisms 1809-1815, 1815-1839
marriages and burials 1809-
1815,1815-1840

St. Patrick's
Combined register 1700-1704 plus
 some 1771 entries and one 1774
marriage

5.3   Presbyterian Records

The Presbyterian records relating to Limerick are limited. The earliest locally
held records are from 1829.   Limerick Ancestry holds records from this date
for the Glentworth St. Church. The Presbyterian Historical Society of Ireland

in Belfast holds marriage records for Limerick for the periods 1813-1841 and 1846-1892. This society also has a communicants roll book for 1844-1910. (see chapter 15).

Some useful background reference books on the presbyterian church include: *Presbyterians in Limerick* by Hugh Lilburn Limerick 1959. This book is also available on microfilm from the LDS.

History of Presbyterianism in Dublin and in the south and west of Ireland by C.H.Irwin, published London, Hodder & Smith, 1890 also gives good background information on this particular church.

The PRONI has some Presbyterian records relating to Limerick. You should access the PRONI website for a list of microfilmed records held (see chapter 15).

5.4   Methodist Records

The earliest Limerick reference to Methodism is to a Rev. George Whitfield preaching in St. Mary's cathedral in 1739. John Wesley, the founder of Methodism held the first Irish Conference in Limerick in 1752 (see 'John Wesley in Ireland with particular reference to North Munster' in NMAJ 2000 40 p. 63-72 by Dudley Levistone Cooney). Methodist chapels were located in Adare, Ballingrane, Courtmatrix, Killeheen, Limerick, Pallaskenry and Rathkeale.

The majority were members of the Established Church (i.e. Church of Ireland) so the records would have been entered in their parish registers. Marriage and burial records up to 1782 are found in the Church of Ireland. Marriage and burial records of members of the primitive Wesleyan Methodist Society up to 1878 can also be found in the registers of the Church of Ireland. The keeping of baptismal registers did not formally commence until after 1817/18. Before that, search Church of Ireland records. Limerick Ancestry holds baptismal records from 1824. The PRONI holds records for the period 1824-1846 for the Limerick circuit. For further reading on this church see Robert Herbert's article in NMAJ 1944, 4 (2) p. 79 which lists members.

The main Limerick community to embrace Methodism was the Palatines (see 5.5). Many of these Palatine families became Methodist and societies were formed in the areas they occupied.

Readers should refer to *Irish Methodists-where do I start* by Steven C. ffeary-Smyrl [Irish Genealogists series No. 1] Dublin, Council of Irish Genealogist

Organisations, 2000 for a succinct guide to this church.
The History of Methodism in Ireland by C.H. Crookshank pub. Belfast, R.S. Allen, 1885-1888, should also be consulted for a more comprehensive history of this church and its records. A former rector in Adare, Dudley Levistone Cooney has published *Methodists in Ireland- a short history* pub. Dublin, Columba Press, 2001. Note that *Thom's Irish Almanac and Official Directory for the year 1847* is quite useful as it locates members of the Methodist Church around this period.

---

5. 5   Palatines

The Palatines emigrated around 1709 from the Rhine Palatine region of Germany and were encouraged to settle in Ireland. There were several Palatine settlements in Limerick, notably on the Southwell estate near Rathkeale, where they established the villages of Castlematrix, Killeheen and Ballingrane and on the Oliver estate near Kilfinane where they established the villages of Ballyriggan, Ballyorgan and Glenosheen. The founder of Methodism, John Wesley said of them in 1760: *'There is no cursing or swearing, no Sabbath breaking, no drunkeness, no ale-houses in any of them'*

The Palatine way of industrious living endured well into the nineteenth century. Their distinct names include the following: Baker, Bovenizer, Doupe, Le Gear, Mees, Miller, Teskey, Shier and Sparling. There are also names like Alton, Barkman, Corneille, Fitzell, Gilliard, Heavenor, Micks and Switzer.

Books on Limerick Palatine families include:
People Make Places - the story of the Irish Palatines by Patrick J. O'Connor Oireacht na Mumhan, 1989. *Palatine Families of Ireland*, Hank Jones, California, 1965. Dudley Levistone Cooney has published *The Irish Palatines,* Adare 1998.

There are also many other sources   including Richard Hayes' article 'The German Colony In Limerick' (NMAJ 1937, 1 p. 42-53) and a short article by Bob Reece called 'Some Limerick Palatines' in the OLJ (1988, no. 23, p. 161-164). Wider accounts of the Palatines in Ireland and North America include Carolyn A. Heald's *The Irish Palatines in Ontario: Religion, Ethnicity, and Rural Migration* concerns the Palatines from Germany who settled in Ireland in the early 1700's and there descendants who immigrated to Ontario. *Ireland and the centenary of American Methodism* by Rev. William Crook published London 1866 deals with the part played by Irish Palatines in the foundation of the American church (see above Methodist records).

The LDS Family History Library has Collections on the Palatines (film no.100212) compiled by Tenison Groves. This is a microfilm of ms. 540 held at the GO. It contains a history of Palatine migration into Limerick County in 1709, Irish Palatine surnames as well as a list of Protestants and Papists in Limerick Diocese 1766.

It is also well worth looking at Arthur Young's *Tour of Ireland 1776-1779* for a contemporary account of the distinctive way of life of the early settlers and their gradual absorption into the Irish way of life. The historian Richard Ferrar said of them in 1780,

' *The Palatines preserve their language, but it is declining....they have by degrees left off their sour krout, and feed on potatoes, butter, milk, oaten and wheaten bread'*

Today their numbers are greatly reduced but there is a Palatine Society in Rathkeale run by Austin Bovenizer. Further information on the Palatines can be found on the web at *www.local.ie/content/28303.shtml*

Also at the Dubery family website
http://www.geocities.com/Area51/Station/9230/Genealogy/index.htm
there are extensive transcriptions of LDS microfilmed birth and christening records of Irish Palatine families. Births are covered from 1742- 1750 and christenings from 1791-1810.

---

5. 6   Jews

Most of the Jews in Limerick immigrated from Lithuania around the 1870's and it was always a small community. Their history in Limerick is not a particular source of pride for Limerick people. They were the victims of an economic boycott in 1904 when life was made intolerable for them. The writer Standish O'Grady said of them:

> *'These Limerick Jews seem to be a very harmless body, neither money-lenders nor extortioners, just traders in clothes, and selling the same at no more profit than is permitted'*

The Jewish surnames of Limerick between 1847 and 1938 were Arinon, Blonde, Clein, Cropman, Fine, Genese, Gewurtz, Goldberg, Gould, Graff, Greenfield, Jaffe, Jerome, Kaitcher, Leone, Levin, Moizel, Sandler, Siev, Tobin, Toohey and Weinronk.

There are two excellent accounts of the Jews in Ireland. One is Richard Hymans book *The Jews in Ireland from the earliest times to 1910*, Irish University Press, Shannon 1972. The other is *The Jews in Twentieth Century*

Ireland by Dermot Keogh, Cork O.U.P. 1998. Aspects of the 1904 pogrom are covered by Pat Feeley in the OLJ Summer 1982 p. 18-24. There is a Jewish graveyard in Kilmurry, near Limerick city which has been restored. One should also visit the Irish Jewish Museum at 3-4 Walworth Road, South Circular Road, Dublin.

---

5. 7   Quakers

Quaker meeting houses were established in the principal Munster towns of Cork, Limerick and Waterford after the arrival of the Quakers in Ireland in the mid-17th century. The Quakers were excellent record keepers and their records are arguably the best of all of the denominations that exist in Ireland. Their records relating to Limerick are preserved in the Dublin Friends Historical Library at Swanbrook House, Morehampton Rd., Dublin 4. Birth, marriage and death records exist for Limerick from 1623-1863. An excellent account of the Irish Quaker records is given by Richard Harrison in the chapter *'Irish Quaker Records'* in *Irish Church Records'* Flyleaf Press, (Dublin, 2001). Olive Goodbody's (ed.) *The Guide To Irish Quaker Records* pub. Dublin, IMC, 1967 lists abstracts of Quaker wills. The LDS have register transcripts 1619-1863 of the Limerick Monthly Meeting on film (no.571396). The Quakers were, and are, significantly involved in charitable work and their records include about 3000 letters, journals, diaries and correspondence relating to the work carried out by Quakers during the famine period.

The National Library also holds microfilm copies of birth, marriage and death records arranged under name of the area of the monthly meeting.. See also OCM 14:564-626 and LDS film 571396. There is a very interesting article in the OLJ by Rob Goodbody called 'Limerick Quakers and Famine Relief' (OLJ Famine edition, 1995 p. 68-74). See also 'The Quakers in Limerick' by Emilie M. Bennis in OLJ .30 1993 p. 4-6 and there is also a more recent article by Phil Lovett in the Summer 2001 edition, p. 3-9. A miscellaneous source for this religion is the Brown papers edited by Edward McLysaght in *An. Hib.* no.15 1944. These relate to the Quaker family of Pearce and to other Limerick Quakers. The Quaker graveyard at Ballinacurra near Punch's Cross, Limerick is also well worth visiting.

8.8   Congregationalists

There are some records filmed by the LDS for the Congregational Church of Christ in Limerick –film no.496750. They are baptisms 1817-1820, births 1821-1871, marriages 1819-1871.

Chapter 6   Civil Registration

The civil registration of all births, marriages and deaths in Ireland began on the 1st January 1864. However, non-Catholic marriages have been registered since the 1st April 1845. All civil registrations are held by the General Registers Office in Dublin where they are arranged alphabetically in yearly indexed volumes. Each volume gives the surname, forename, superintendent registrar's district and a reference which consists of a volume number and page number. On production of a reference a photocopy of a register entry or a full certificate will be issued for a set fee.

The Superintendent Registrar's District is based on the Poor Law Union districts (See chapter 3 Land Records) which were formed under the Poor Law Act of 1838. Limerick is divided into eight Superintendent Registrars Districts (Poor Law Unions) namely Croom, Glin, Kilmallock, Limerick, Mitchelstown, Newcastle, Rathkeale and Tipperary. It is from these districts that the master index of births, marriages and deaths is compiled.

Some registrar's districts were later amalgamated with other districts, in the case of Limerick the registration district of Glin was amalgamated with Rathkeale in January 1892. When consulting the indexes to births, marriages and deaths it should be remembered that the volumes are arranged as follows:

Births:
• 1864 to 1877 are yearly and indexed alphabetically.
• 1878 to 1902 are yearly, subdivided quarterly and indexed alphabetically.
• 1903 to 1927 and 1933 are arranged in volumes, alphabetically by surname.
• 1928 to 1965 are yearly, subdivided quarterly and indexed alphabetically.
• 1966 to 1995 are arranged in volumes, alphabetically by surname.

Marriages:
• 1845 to 1875 are yearly and indexed alphabetically.
• 1876 to 1965 are yearly, subdivided quarterly and indexed alphabetically.
• 1966 to 1995 are arranged in volumes, alphabetically by surname.

Deaths:
• 1864 to 1874 are yearly and indexed alphabetically.
• 1875 to 1965 are yearly, subdivided quarterly and indexed alphabetically.
• 1966 to 1995 are arranged in volumes, alphabetically by surname.

As the registration of births, marriages and deaths will not always occur in the same quarter as the event, subsequent quarters should also be consulted. Late

—— James.	Enniscorthy	14	724
—— Michael.	Baltinglass	2	523
HAYDUAN, Thomas.	Mullingar	8	364
HAYES. Aiden John.	Wexford	4	1057
.—— Alice.	Newry	16	777
—— Allice.	Waterford	19	912
—— Ally.	Cashel	8	529
—— Anne.	Clonakilty	20	82
—— Anne Jane.	Dublin, South	12	675
—— Anne Maria.	Listowel	10	499
—— Bartholemew.	Skibbereen	15	557
—— Bridget.	Clonmel	14	670
—— Bridget.	Ennistimon	4	313
—— Bridget.	Clonakilty	5	103
—— Bridget.	Ennis	9	263
—— Bridget.	Dunmanway	10	246
—— Bridget.	Kanturk	10	296
—— Bridget.	Killarney	5	387
—— Bridget.	Mallow	5	629
—— Bridget.	Thurles	18	642
—— Bridget.	Kilmallock	15	344
—— Bridget.	Limerick	15	422
—— Bryan.	Nenagh	18	563
—— Catharine.	Limerick	15	408
.—— Catharine.	Limerick	15	417
—— Catherine.	Clonakilty	5	110
—— Catherine.	Roscommon	8	412
—— Catherine.	Limerick	5	522
—— Catherine.	Dublin, South	2	741
—— Catherine.	Enniscorthy	14	725
—— Catherine.	Middleton	14	790
—— Catherine.	Dublin, South	17	643
—— Catherine.	Clonakilty	10	72
—— Catherine.	Clonakilty	15	75
—— Catherine.	Listowel	15	448
—— Catherine.	Tipperary	3	759
—— Catherine.	Limerick	5	488
—— Catherine.	Urlingford	18	693
—— Catherine.	Mallow	10	564

**A page from the birth indexes for 1866 showing surname, forename,
registration district and relevant reference numbers**

registrations can also be found in the back pages of each index volume.

To establish the relevant Superintendent Registrar's District (Poor Law Union) for a specific area either of the following should be consulted:
General Alphabetical Index to the Townlands and Towns, Parishes and Baronies of Ireland (based on the Census of Ireland for the year 1851) Published by Alexander Thom Dublin 1861 and Genealogical Publishing Baltimore, 1984).
Townlands in Poor Law Unions - A reprint of the Poor Law Union pamphlets of the General Registrar's Office by George B. Handran (see chapter 2 Administrative Divisions).

On obtaining a photocopy of a register entry one can expect to find the following details:

Births – Date and place of birth, name and sex of child, name, address and occupation of father, name and maiden name of mother, name and address of informant, date and signature of registrar.

Marriage – Date and place of marriage, name, age, occupation and marital status (Spinster, bachelor, widow, widower) of bride and groom, address at time of marriage, name and occupation of father of bride and groom, names of witnesses and name of cleric. After 1950 additional information is given such as date of birth, future address and mother's name.

Death – Date and place of death, name of deceased, sex, marital status, age, occupation, cause of death, name and address of informant, date and signature of registrar.

Civil registration records also held at the GRO along with the above are:

• Births of Irish subjects which, took place at sea from 1864.
• Deaths of Irish subjects, which took place at sea from 1864.
• Births, marriages and deaths of Irish subjects serving in the British Army
  abroad from 1880.
• Births of Irish subjects abroad from 1864. Such births had to be notified
  to the relevant British Council abroad.

Remember to check variations in spelling of the name you are seeking, e.g. search for variations with and without the O' or Mac' and also sound-alike variations.

Limerick Wills, 1615-1800.	131

	Date of Probate.
Sexton, Patrick (baker), Limerick	*1799
,, Richard (burgess), Limerick	1700
Shaghnessy, Francis, Cappagh	1728
,, Teige McDavid	1700
Shaghanassey, Maurice, Darriry, co. Limerick ..	1765
Shaughnessy, John .. '	1795
Shaughnissy, William (shopkeeper), Limerick ..	1744
Shea, William (house carpenter), North Suburbs of Lim'k	1777
Sheahan, Martin (farmer), Moig, Shanagolden, co. Lim'k	1794
,, Timothy (farmer), Romer, Adare, co. Limerick	1800
Sheanan, Connor (parish priest), Kildimo Kenry, co. Limerick	1713
Sheehy, John (farmer), Shanaclough, co. Limerick ..	1798
Sheghan, John (gent.), Knockbrack, co. Limerick ..	1729
Shelton, John (gent.), Ross, co. Limerick	1734
Sheppard, John (woollen draper), Limerick.. ..	1767
Shine, Cornelius (gent.), New Castle, co. Limerick ..	1775
Shirley, Grizell, Limerick	1686
Siffrett, Woulkmor (chandler), Limerick	1716
Singeon, Jasper (farmer), Ballygarrane, co. Limerick..	1790
Slater, James (tanner), Limerick	1718
Smith, Robert (alderman), Limerick	1703
,, William (gent.), Limerick	1727
Smithe, Arthur (chandler), Limerick	1684
Smyth, John, Chandrenagor, 39th Regiment of Foot ..	1765
,, Samuel (Rev.), Limerick	1732
Southwell, Elizabeth (Dame, widow), Castlematres, Rathkeale, co. Limerick	1705
,, Richard (esq.), Callow, co. Limerick ..	1679
Spencer, Giles (gent.), Limerick	1692
Spierin, Luke (gent.), Cappaugh, co. Limerick ..	1728
,, Mathew (gent.), Rower, co. Limerick ..	1719
Squibb, Mathew, Limerick	1719
Stanton, Laurence (Rev.)	1779
Starkey, Sarah (widow), Limerick	1785
Starr, John, Mountpleasant, Kenry, co. Limerick ..	1782
,, William, Shannougrove, Kenry, co. Limerick (*copy*)	1778
Steeres, Richard (Rev.), Fedamore, co. Limerick ..	1764
Stokes, John (gent.), Ballinlonderrig, co. Limerick ..	1682
Stondon, Edmond (farmer), North Liberties of Limerick	1786

A page from *Indexes to Irish Wills* edited by Phillimore and Thrift, originally published in five volumes from 1909 to 1920, reprinted(five volumes in one) by Genealogical Publishing Co. Inc. 1997.

Chapter 7 Wills, Administrations & Marriage License Bonds

Wills are a rich source for the genealogist. As well as being social documents in their own right, wills can provide details of family relationships, can trace the disposition of family property and can also be used to estimate a family's wealth.

Until 1857 testamentary jurisdiction in Ireland was exercised by the Church of Ireland which was until then the formal state church of the country. As part of this formal role courts run by the Church of Ireland decided whether a will was valid, and distributed property in the absence of a will. The wills were proved in the Consistorial Court of the diocese in which the testator lived. However if the estate had a value of over £5 in a second diocese then probate was the responsibility of the Prerogative Court of the Archbishop of Armagh which sat in Dublin. There are separate indexes of wills and administrations for both the Consistorial (diocesan) Court and the Prerogative Court. If the name you are looking for is not found among the indexes of the consistorial court then search indexes in the adjacent dioceses and the next higher jurisdiction, the Church of Ireland province of Armagh. Some of these indexes have been published in Vicar's *Index to the Prerogative Wills of Ireland 1536-1810* (pub. Dublin, E. Ponsonby, 1967).

In 1858 these church courts were replaced by the Principal and District Registries of the Probate Court. There is a consolidated index in the NAI for the period 1858-77. There are indexes in the Calendar of Wills and Administrations (one or two volumes per year), which are available for consultation in the NAI. The calendar of wills provides the name, address and occupation of the deceased, place of death, names and addresses of grantees of probate or administration and the relationship to the deceased. You will also be able to get the exact date of probate and the value of the estate. These Calendars of Wills are on open access in the NAI.

In 1867 the records of wills and administrations from the Consistorial and Prerogative Courts were transferred to the then Public Records Office (NAI). These records together with the post-1857 testamentary material of the principal registry were destroyed in a fire at this repository in 1922. Since then the National Archives has been acquiring copy wills. Other institutions like the Royal Irish Academy, the Society of Friends and the Registry of Deeds also have important collections (See chapter 13).). Some Quaker Wills were published in Goodbody and Eustace's *Quaker Records, Dublin, Abstract of*

Wills, Dublin, IMC, 1957. An index to the Will abstracts in the Genealogical Office are listed in *Guide to The Genealogical Office, Dublin* (IMC 1998).

County Limerick is in the Church of Ireland dioceses of Emly and Limerick with a few parishes in Cashel, Killaloe and Cloyne. The guide to Church of Ireland parish records in Chapter 5 shows the diocese to which each civil parish belonged. The Wills of residents of each diocese were usually proven within that diocese unless they came under the jurisdiction of the Prerogative court.

Pre-1858 Wills and Administrations:
Indexes of Wills up to 1800 have been compiled by Gertrude Thrift and published as *Indexes to Irish Wills* by Phillimore. This includes Killaloe diocesan fragments from 1653-1858. These have been republished by Genealogical Publishing Co. (1997). Volume 3 of the Indexes covers Cashel, Emly and Limerick diocesan area and is now available on CD-ROM from A.J.Morris Genealogy, see: *www.genealogy.org/~ajmorris/catalog/00445.htm*

In relation to pre -1858 Limerick Wills, the Westropp manuscripts in the Royal Irish Academy have many abstracts of wills and administrations from counties Limerick and Clare- ms. vol. 3A39. There are also indexes for the period 1615-1858.

Post-1858 Wills and Administrations:
The District Registry of Limerick was responsible for proving Wills in this area. The surviving records are kept in the NAI and are also on microfilm in Limerick Ancestry .
Limerick District Will Books (1858-88) are in the NAI and LDS film 1009467.
Limerick District Will Books (1858-1894) in NAI and LDS film 100951-4.
Richard Hayes articles in the NMAJ 1936-39, 1, p.163-168 and NMAJ 1940-41, 2, p.71-75 deals with 'Some Old Limerick Wills'.

Will abstracts and notes on the Adams family of Counties Cork and Limerick are in the Genealogical Office ms.450 and 451-455. Some Catholic episcopal Wills for Drs. O'Keefe 1720-1737 and Conway 1779-1796 (from prerogative Wills) are recorded in *Arch. Hib.* 1914, 3 p. 195. The Will of Andrew Walsh, an eighteenth century printer is recorded in *N.Mun.ArchSoc.Jrnl* 1911, 11 (1) p.44-46 . This is also available on LDS film (film 257780 and 100148). Canon John Begley's 3 volume *History of the Diocese of Limerick* is also another printed source (reprinted by O'Brien Toomey, Limerick,1993).
Readers are also advised to consult Rosemary ffolliott's and Eileen O'Byrne's article on Wills and Administrations in the book *Irish Genealogy – a record finder* edited by D. F. Begley published in Dublin by Heraldic Artists, 1987.

THOMAS ARTHUR, Doctor of Physic.

I appoint my wife, Christian Arthur, sole executrix.

I bequeath unto said wife all my lands of Tullaghedy, containing two plowes in Ormond, in the countie of Tipperarie, and the lands of Mayne, Co. Galway, and all other my lands in sd countie of Galway now in lease to Henry Davis and enjoyed by him and his assigns by virtue thereof for several years past. To hold the same to said Christian for and during her life. I also bequeath and devise to my wife Christian Arthur all the benefit and advantage which I have or may expect in any land, tenements and heredts by virtue of any clause or proviso in the Act of settlement or Explanation in my behalf as nominee or otherwise the same to be held by sd Christian during her life.

To my brother Richard Arthur £6 annually.

I remit and release to my son-in-law Nicholas Comyn whatever debt is due to me of him by bond or otherwise. I further bequeath to my daughter Christian, wife of said Nicholas, the moiety of Newstoune in Co. Carlow and the debt and mortgage thereof due from the Duke of Ormond.

Whereas I owned unto my son-in-law Daniel Arthur the sum of £100 which remained of my daughter Anstace Arthur, his wife's portion, to which sum I paid by order from said Daniel unto John Arthur of Dublin deceased, my son-in-law, and took his bond for the same, I do hereby appoint executors to deliver sd bond to sd Daniel Arthur.

To grandchildren, Daniel Arthur the younger, Eleanor Arthur and Anstace Arthur, children of the sd Daniel Arthur, my son-in-law, and of my daughter Anstace decd., the other moiety of said debt and mortgage of Newstoune from the Duke of Ormond to me.

To wife all other my goods and chattels.

31 Dec. 1674.

CODICIL. My further will is that William Arthur FfitzJohn of Dublin, in case he be living, be my heir, and that after the death of my wife and exectrx and after the time before by my last will limited do hold and enjoy all my estate of inheritance within the kingdom of Ireland to him the sd William Arthur and the heirs male of his body, and for want of such heirs, sd estate of inheritance shall descend to my grandson, Thomas Arthur FfitzJohn and his heirs male, and from want of such heirs, to Thomas Arthur of Limerick Doctor of Physic and his heirs male, and for want of such heirs my said estate of inheritance shall descend and come unto to the right heirs of me, the said Thomas Arthur FfitzWilliam and their heirs for ever. And I do declare for the several injuries done unto me by my sonne John Arthur and my daughter Demphna his wife and her disrespect unto me that I was intended not to transfer any of my estate upon their issue, but by the earnest entreaty of my now wife Christian I have been enduced to make this provision for them. I wish that my wife be recommended as by my last will and request to the favour of the Right Honble the Countess of Mount Alexander, doubting not that she will answer her in all her just demands and reasonable desires.

Dated 2 Jan 1674

Proved 27Jan 1674.

4. This document was destroyed in the fire at the P.R.O. during the civil conflict of 1922. There is a short summary of it in the 15th Annual Report, Records of Ireland (Act of Settlement Book).

5. It is generally but wrongly stated that he died in 1663, the assumption being made that the year of his death coincided with the last year chronicled in his *Diary*.

A sample of a Will dated 1674 from NMAJ 1(3) 1938

Marriage Licence Bonds

A legal marriage required the publication of 'Banns', i.e. a notice declaring an intention of a couple to marry. An alternative to publishing the banns was to purchase a licence to marry. Before the Bishop of the diocese issued such a licence, the groom and another person lodged a sum of money as surety that there was no obstacle to the marriage. Usually the person with the groom was a relative of the bride.

Indexes of marriage licence bonds survive and are arranged by diocese and have some abstracts. The NAI has marriage licences for the Cashel diocese 1840-1845; and for Cashel and Emly diocese 1644-1857 (LDS film 101027); and for the diocese of Killaloe 1691-1845 (LDS film 100869). The LDS Family History Library has an index to the marriages in Co. Limerick before 1st April 1845 as shown by the Church of Ireland registers. This has already been dealt with in chapter 5. The LDS has Act Books 1840-1845 which list marriage licences for the Diocese of Cashel and Emly (film no.101027). The originals of these are held in the RCBL. The GO has marriage licences for the Diocese of Killaloe 1680-1762 (GO Ms. 688: LDS film no.100239). Some of this material can be accessed at *http://home.att.net/-labaths* (1680-1720 and 1760-1762).

There are some marriage licence bonds transcribed - see R.T.D. Fitzgerald's 'Killaloe Marriage License Bonds 1680-1720 and 1760-1762' in *Ir.Gen.* 1978 5 (5) p. 580-590. These were in manuscripts purchased by the British Museum in 1881 from the noted Limerick historian Maurice Lenihan. 'Killaloe Marriage License Grants 1776-1845' by E.J.McAuliffe are in *Ir.Gen.* 1979 5 (6) p. 710-719. Hardly any records have survived of the dispensations in the Catholic church. The only known examples in Limerick are to be found in the early records of Croom parish. However, it seems likely that these dispensations were for an area much wider than Croom, as they are simply too numerous to represent the needs of that parish.

Chapter 8   Grave Records and Inscriptions

Gravestone inscriptions, where they exist, are a valuable genealogical source as they can provide information on several generations of a family. Even the type of gravestone erected can give an insight into the economic and social standing of a family. Locating gravestones can sometimes be a difficult process. Many Irish families had particular burial grounds that were remote from their homes or parishes. Also members of one family could be buried in different places. Where feasible, it is useful to ask living relatives the name and location of the cemetery or cemeteries where deceased family members are buried. Otherwise, it is a process of checking the local graveyards, and then widening the search to other places associated with the family in previous generations. Information on places of burial is also found in newspaper obituaries (see Chapter 12) and remembrance cards.

In Ireland it is important to note that Catholics and Protestants were often buried in one graveyard. So the older Church of Ireland graveyards can be a source for some Catholic families. It is not uncommon for the Church of Ireland graveyard to be a burial place for other Protestant denominations such as Presbyterian and Methodist.

In Co. Limerick the names of the graveyards may be known locally by a name different to that stated on maps. The old Church of Ireland graveyard in Tuogh is now considered to be in the Cappamore parish, which is the modern name for Tuogh. The Catholic graveyard of Doon parish is in the townland of Liscaugh but is referred to as Doon. Also some burial places marked on maps are too old to be of any value for ancestry research. The burial ground marked at Bilboa in the parish of Cappamore is apparently just an empty field. Likewise the burial grounds of Kilduffahoo and Kylenanny are devoid of any physical indicators of burial.

A trip to a full graveyard can be an end in itself. Poring over the old inscriptions can make you feel in touch with by-gone ancestors. A sense of the impermanence of all generations can be felt. Gravestones offer more than just a mere date of death. They can often give information on relationships (son of …beloved wife of etc), places of residence and occupations. The legibility of the headstones can vary especially as some stones weathered easily. Time, weather and tree roots may all have taken their toll on the stones. In order to read old inscriptions chalk or clumps of wet grass rubbed along the lines are all that is required. Do not use any chemical agents especially as there are preservation orders on many old graveyards. If cleaning needs to be done,

use only soft brushes and water. Ivy should not be removed if it is seen to be keeping the stone together! Also take a camera and notebook to record your findings.
You should not be disappointed if you fail to find a headstone for your particular family. There were many families who could not afford a headstone. You may instead come across just a simple iron cross or maybe a crude stone. There may be no other identifying mark to testify to earlier generations.

Inscriptions for the following Limerick graveyards are available:

Abbeyfeale:
Some abstracts in OCM.
Abington:
List of inscriptions held by LA
Adare:
Memorials of Adare Manor by Caroline, Countess of Dunraven with historical notices of Adare by her son the Earl of Dunraven, printed for private circulation Oxford 1865.
Ardagh:
'The headstone inscriptions of Ardagh cemetery' by Jerry McMahon in NMAJ 1995, 36 , p. 3-60
Ardcanny:
List of inscriptions in *Ir .Anc.* 1977, 1, p. 3-5 transcribed by M.J. Dore
Ardpatrick:
Reflections, Historical and Topographical on Ardpatrick, Co.Limerick, by John Fleming, 1979
Askeaton:
List of inscriptions in IGRS collection, GO, NAI, RCBL.
Athlacca:
Dromin Athlacca by Mainchin Seoighe, 1978 published by Glor na nGael, Ath Leacach
Ballinacurra:
(Quaker) gravestone inscriptions in Margaret Lyddy's, *St.Joseph's Parish* n.d.
Ballinard:
LGDJ 1990, p. 82-86 (Herbertstown)
Ballingaddy:
See Kilmallock
Ballingarry:
Records of Ballingarry, by Rev. G. F. Hamilton, 1930 Limerick, McKern's
Ballingirlough:
List of inscriptions in *The Dawn* 1980 , no.5 p. 90
Bruff:
List of inscriptions in *The Dawn*, 1980 no. 5 p. 86-89 and 1986 no.6 p. 142-151 (Church of Ireland inscriptions).

Bruree:
Bru Ri, the history of the Bruree district by Mainchin Seoighe published by Cumann Forbartha Bhru Ri in 1972, inscriptions also held by LA.
Bulgaden:
Abstracts held by LA
Cahercorney:
Cahercorney graveyard in LGDJ 2000 no. 11, p. 102-107
Castleconnell:
see Stradbally
Castletown Conyers:
'Memorial inscriptions from Castletown Conyers' by K.T. Vaughan, unpublished project for UCD Certificate in Genealogy, 1999
Darragh:
Inscriptions held by LA - see *Glenroe-Ballyorgan Parish God's Acre 1997* published by Glenroe/Ballyorgan graves committee (covers Darragh, Glenroe and Kilflynn graveyards).
Donoughmore:
Transcribed by Tom Toomey, held by LA
Dromin:
Dromin Athlacca, by Mainchin Seoighe, 1978 Glor na nGael, Ath Leacach
Effin:
Inscriptions held by LA
Elton:
Inscriptions held by LA
Glenbrohane:
Graveyard inscriptions of Ballingarry and Laraghlawe churchyards, parish of Glenbrohane, Garryspillane, Co. Limerick 1998 published by the Glenbrohane Community Association
Glenroe/Ballyorgan:
Inscriptions held by LA and see Darragh above .
Glin:
Held in Limerick County Library
Grange:
(near Newcastle): *Ir.Anc.* 1978, 10 (1) p. 49-51 transcribed by M.J. Dore
Grange:
(near Bruff) in the LGDJ 1989 no.5 p. 75-81
Herbertstown:(Ballynamona & Kilcullane)
Some transcriptions in LGDJ 2000 no11 p.108-110.
Hospital:
LGDJ 1994 no.8 p. 115-124 also 1996 no.9 p. 85-92 and 1998 no.10 p. 63-70
Kilbehenny:
List of inscriptions in *Ir.Gen.* 1954 2 (11) p. 349-354
Kilfinane:
(RC and C of I): inscriptions held by LA.

Kilmallock:
(RC and C of I) and Ballingaddy: FAS list held by LA;   *also Bru Ri: The history of the Bruree district,* by Mainchin Seoighe, 1973
Kilpeacon:
Kilpeacon Parish Church by Niall Johnston 1990 contains some memorials.
Also see Westropp T.J. in *Journal of the Association for the Preservation of the Memorials of the Dead* 1900 4 (4) p. 440-442.
Kilquane:
(in Parteen, Co. Clare, Limerick diocese) : Sliabh Aughty Journal 1994
Knockaney:
Knockaney, Co.Limerick by Michael Quinlan in the LGDJ 1987 p. 88-99
and 1988 p. 69-79
Knockpatrick:
Knockpatrick Churchyard by T.J.Westropp in *Jrnl. Of the Assoc. for the Preservation of the Memorials of the Dead* 1905 6 (1) p. 384-385 and see also 'An Irish inscription in Knockpatrick churchyard' by J.Begley in *N.Mun. Arch.Soc.Jrnl* .1911, 1 (4) p. 253-254 See also Shanagolden
Laraghlawe:
see Glenbrohane
Limerick City:
St. Mary's Cathedral in *The Monuments of St. Mary's* by Rev. M. J. Talbot, Limerick, 1976. St. John's Church of Ireland typescript copy held by LA .
St. Munchin's Church of Ireland, inscriptions held by LA.
There are also some inscriptions recorded for Limerick from tombstones by M.R. Lascelles-Kelly. These are available on microfilm from the LDS and were copied from an original transcript at the GO ms. 564, 682.
Lough Gur:
LGDJ 1985, p. 55-60
Mount St. Laurence:
LDS film no.1419439. Limerick Ancestry has a computerised index from 1855 to 1955.
Mountcollins:
Some abstracts in OCM.
Mungret:
Mungret inscriptions held locally by John O'Connor
Nantinan:
List of inscriptions in *Ir.Anc.* 1980, 12 (1+2) p. 53-62 transcribed by M.J. Dore
Patrickswell (Lough Gur):
'Patrickswell Graveyard' by Michael Quinlan in LGDJ March 1986 p. 71-79
Plassey:
List of inscriptions in GO ms.622
Raheen (Ballineety):
Transcribed by TomToomey and Maurice FitzGerald, held in Limerick city library .

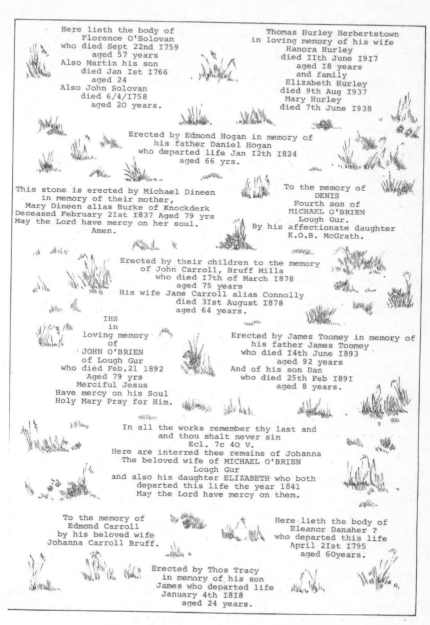

Here lieth the body of
Florence O'Solovan
who died Sept 22nd I759
aged 57 years
Also Martin his son
died Jan Ist I766
aged 24
Also John Solovan
died 6/4/I758
aged 20 years.

Thomas Hurley Herbertstown
in loving memory of his wife
Hanora Hurley
died IIth June I9I7
aged I8 years
and family
Elizabeth Hurley
died 9th Aug I937
Mary Hurley
died 7th June I938

Erected by Edmond Hogan in memory of
his father Daniel Hogan
who departed life Jan I2th I824
aged 66 yrs.

This stone is erected by Michael Dineen
in memory of their mother,
Mary Dineen alias Burke of Knockderk
Deceased February 2Ist I837 Aged 79 yrs
May the Lord have mercy on her soul.
Amen.

To the memory of
DENIS
Fourth son of
MICHAEL O'BRIEN
Lough Gur.
By his affectionate daughter
K.O.B. McGrath.

Erected by their children to the memory
of John Carroll, Bruff Mills
who died I7th of March I878
aged 75 years
His wife Jane Carroll alias Connolly
died 3Ist August I878
aged 64 years.

IHS
in
loving memory
of
JOHN O'BRIEN
of Lough Gur
who died Feb.2I I892
Aged 79 yrs
Merciful Jesus
Have mercy on his Soul
Holy Mary Pray for Him.

Erected by James Toomey in memory of
his father James Toomey
who died I4th June I893
aged 92 years
And of his son Dan
who died 25th Feb I89I
aged 8 years.

In all the works remember thy last and
and thou shalt never sin
Ecl. 7c 40 V.
Here are interred thee remains of Johanna
The beloved wife of MICHAEL O'BRIEN
Lough Gur
and also his daughter ELIZABETH who both
departed this life the year 1841
May the Lord have mercy on them.

To the memory of
Edmond Carroll
by his beloved wife
Johanna Carroll Bruff.

Here lieth the body of
Eleanor Danaher ?
who departed this life
April 2Ist I795
aged 60years.

Erected by Thos Tracy
in memory of his son
James who departed life
January 4th I8I8
aged 24 years.

A page from *Patrickswell Graveyard inscriptions*
by Michael Quinlan in the LGDJ March 1986 p. 71-79.

Rathkeale:
Colaiste na Trocaire, Rathkeale, has documented St.Mary's Catholic church graveyard. A copy is held by LA.
M.J. Dore's 'Monumental inscriptions for the Church of Ireland Graveyard' is in *Ir. Anc.* 1982 , 14 (2) p.105-120; and also available at Cathy Labaths website at http://home.att.net/~labaths/limerick.htm.
Robertstown:
See Shanagolden
Shanagolden:
Inscriptions held by LA (includes Knockpatrick, Robertstown and Mt. Pleasant cemeteries)
Stradbally :
List of inscriptions in IGRS collection GO, NAI, RCBL
Tankardstown:
Bru Ri: The history of the Bruree district, by Mainchin Seoighe, 1972 p. 115-129
Templain:
Templain graveyard in *The Dawn* 1980 , no.5 p. 87-89
Towerhill (Cappamore):
Inscriptions by Mary T. Ryan in *Ceapach Mhor* 2000, p.47-51.
Tullybrackey:
'Tullybrackey Graveyard' in *The Dawn* 1988 no. 7 p. 125-146

Grave registers, or registers of burials within a graveyard, or from a particular church are another source but they are not readily available, particularly for the early graveyards. Some are in local custody while others are held by the county council and by Limerick Corporation. The city's Mount St Lawrence cemetery now has a computerised index (see above) that is held by both Limerick Corporation and Limerick Ancestry.

A Guide to Irish parish registers and graveyards is published by Brian Mitchell (Genealogical Pub. Co., Baltimore 1988) but it is not complete. The Limerick County Library holds a copy of the OCM entries (for Mountcollins and Abbeyfeale) in their local studies dept. These are also available from Cork county library service.
Finally, the *Journal of the Association for the Preservation of the Memorials of the Dead* published between 1888 and 1933 (Dublin, Peter Roe) contains hundreds of inscriptions and is indexed by name and place. This journal is held locally by the Limerick City Library and in many other libraries nationally (see chapter 13).

Chapter 9   Newspapers

Old newspapers are another useful source of genealogical material. Irish newspapers appeared from the middle of the eighteenth century. At first they were only a few pages long, published several times per week, and their coverage was mainly targeted at the activities of the gentry and professionals. By the late nineteenth century however, national publications were appearing daily. The first Limerick newspaper was *The Munster Journal* of 1749 followed by *The Limerick Chronicle* in 1768. These papers were much smaller than those of today and they did not appear with the same frequency. As the nineteenth century progressed the papers began to carry more biographical information and also more titles became available. As today, different newspapers were launched to cater for certain economic or political groups. *The Limerick Leader*, which is still in existence, was first published in 1893.

Newspapers are a good source for births, marriage and death announcements and the occasional obituary. They also contain reports of court cases, petitions and other local news which names individuals. If you had a convict ancestor, the old newspapers are a useful source for accounts of trials etc. They also carried many advertisements for local traders. Newspapers reflected the social and economic life of Ireland at the time. The principal drawback to searching the papers is that unless you have a fairly precise date for an event you might have to spend hours (or even days) searching them. This however need not be such an onerous task as one can find endless items of information that give a background to the period of interest to your search.

Most Irish newspapers have been microfilmed, although complete indexes to their contents are still limited. The National Library of Ireland has a major project underway aimed at listing newspaper holdings and identifying priorities for their preservation. This is known as the *NEWSPLAN* project and is in conjunction with the British Library. The book *NEWSPLAN – report on the NEWSPLAN project in Ireland* by James O'Toole published jointly by NLI and BL in 1998 lists county and national newspapers and gives their locations and whether they are available in hardcopy or microfilm. There is an index to the national paper the *Freeman's Journal* which is arranged by date, subject (including surname) and place (subdivided by county). This is held in the NLI. For Limerick papers Rosemary ffolliott has prepared *An Index to Biographical Notices in the Newspapers of Limerick, Ennis, Clonmel and Waterford 1758-1821*. This monumental work is available on microfiche at the NAI and GO. Both Limerick Ancestry and Limerick county library also have copies. Some Limerick papers are included in the abstracts of births, deaths and marriages

Limerick evening post, The. no 1- , 30 Oct 1811-c.Mar 1828. *then:* Limerick evening post and Clare sentinel, The. no 1,452-no 1,908, 14 Mar 1828-17 Dec 1833. Limerick; Ennis. *Prpitr:* Daniel Geary (1811-1827); H. Greene. *Printer:* Joseph Haly. 45cm. 5d (1812). *Freq:* twice weekly (Wed Sat, Mon Thu, Tue Fri). *Subjects:* newspapers; newspapers, twice weekly. *Depts:* auctions, London fashions, excerpts from London papers, agriculture report, notices, advertising. *Cmnts:* The paper did not publish between 06 Apr-23 Oct 1832 and between 29 Mar-02 Aug 1833; from 14 Mar 1828 to 29 Mar 1833, it was published at Limerick and Ennis. This paper is related to The Limerick Star and Evening Post but no mention is made of this connection in the Colindale Library catalogue. The issue no 3 is dated 06 Nov 1811. *Merge:* absorbed The Clare Sentinel. *Loctn:* Limerick Co Lib (1811-1812); Colin no 1,435-1,908 (01 Jan-26 Feb 1828, 14 Mar 1828-06 Apr 1832, 23 Oct 1832-29 Mar, 02 Aug-17 Dec 1833); NLI (30 Oct 1811-29 Dec 1813, 02 Mar 1814-31 Dec 1818, 14 Mar 1828-17 Dec 1833).

An extract from *The Waterloo Directory of Irish Newspapers and Periodicals, 1800-1900* (North Waterloo Academic Press 1986), an excellent guide for details about newspapers, including dates of publication, proprietors and typical content.

in *'O' Kief, Coshe Mang Slieve Lougher, and Upper Blackwater in Ireland: Historical and Genealogical Items relating to North Cork and East Kerry'.* Entries are taken from the *Limerick Chronicle, Gazette, Evening Post, Star and Evening Post, Standard* and *Reporter.*

The Table on page 76 shows the newspaper holdings of the Limerick County Library, Limerick City Library, Limerick Ancestry and the National Library of Ireland. It is also worth mentioning that the British Library holds an extensive collection of Limerick and other Irish county newspapers.

A miscellaneous source is the *Hunt family of Ireland* by Fred J.R.Hunt, which contains newspaper obituaries from the Limerick Chronicle 1778-1854. This is held by the LDS, British film 1364336 items 9-11. (There are also records from the General Advertiser and Limerick Gazette 1804-1879 (LDS 257780) There are newspaper obituaries for the Hunt family extracted from the *Limerick Chronicle* for the period 1806-1854 available on microfilm from the LDS Family History Library (see chapter 15). There are also obituaries from the *Limerick Chronicle* for 1850 on the internet at *http://uk.geocities.com/irishancestralpages/lc19Jan1850.html* and for 1831 at *http://home.att.net/~wexlababe/limerick_chronicle_1831_deaths*

Finally, there is a U.S. publication series that is of enormous value for emigrant advertisements during the nineteenth century. This is *The Search For Missing Friends* (New England Historical Gen. Soc., Boston) which indexes immigrant advertisements (by name and place) placed in the *Boston Pilot* newspaper. These often give the immigrant's home address in Ireland. The advertisements from 1831 to 1920 have been published in 8 volumes to date.

Of JAMES and ELLEN MADDIGAN, natives of the parish of Kildemo, co.'y Limerick. James came to America about 10 or 11 years ago and landed in Quebec - when last heard from he was in New London, Upper Canada. Ellen is daughter to David Maddigan and Mary Kelly, of said parish of Kildemo. Any information respecting them will be thankfully received by Michael Maddigan, Northfield, Ms.

A typical entry in *The Search for Missing Friends.*

Newspaper	Limerick County Library	Limerick City Library	Limerick Ancestry	National Library of Ireland
Limerick Chronicle		1781 - to date(gaps)	1783 - 1831	1771 - to date(gaps)
Limerick & Clare Examiner				1846 - 1855
Limerick Echo	1923 - 1947			1898 - 1947
Limerick Evening Post	1811 - 1818	1811 - 1818		1811 - 1818
Limerick Gazette(General Advertiser)		1806 - 1820		
Limerick Guardian				1833
Limerick Herald*				1831 - 1835
Limerick Journal				1784
Limerick Leader	1893 - 1999	1893 - to date		1893 - to date
Limerick News				1822 - 1823
Limerick People				1917
Limerick Reporter	1871- 72, 1895	1840 - 1869(gaps)		1839 - 1896
Limerick Standard				1837 - 1841
Limerick Star & Evening Post				1835, 1836
Limerick Times	1834 - 37			1834-37
Limerick Weekly Echo				1921 - 1985
Munster Journal	1749 - 1784	1749 - 1762, 1784		
Munster News		1851 - 1900		

*continued as the Limerick Evening Herald

Chapter 10   Commercial Directories

In the eighteenth and nineteenth century directories of traders, professionals and gentry were published for various towns. They are now an important source for anyone undertaking genealogical research on merchant and professional families, or for those holding public office. The early works tended to list only nobility, gentry and professionals. However as trades became more established they too were listed. The directories can mainly be used to identify ancestors of an upper and middle class background. They can also be used for trades people e.g., coopers, spirit merchants, breeches makers etc. Limerick has the proud distinction of being the first provincial city to issue a directory. John Ferrar produced this in 1769. It lists city traders such as salt-boiler, brush-maker, grocer and tinsman. Names associated with Limerick such as Bennis, Bourke and Barry figure prominently.(see p.78)

Richard Lucas' *General Directory of the Kingdom of Ireland* followed Ferrar's directory in 1788. The nobility and clergy figure strongly but there is also a more in-depth description of tradespeople. There are 30 entries for tallow chandlers and soap boilers. Slater's *Topography and Itinerary of the counties of Ireland* which appeared in 1806 again lists the gentry and their principal 'seats' or residences. This was followed by Holden's *Triennial directory of Limerick* in 1809. Next came Pigot's *Directory of Castleconnell, Kilmallock, Limerick, Newcastle and Rathkeale* which was published in 1824. Slater's *Directory of Adare, Bruff, Castleconnell and O'Brien's Bridge, Croom, Kilmallock, Limerick, Newcastle and Rathkeale* appeared in 1846 and 1856. *Bassett's directory* appeared in 1866 and Slater's again in 1870. Coverage became more extensive towards the end of the nineteenth century. Bassett's was published again for the period 1875-76 and 1880-81. This directory listed the following towns and villages; Abbeyfeale, Adare, Ardagh, Ashford, Askeaton, Athea, Broadford, Bruff, Caherconlish, Castleconnell, Croom, Drumcollogher, Foynes, Glin, Hospital, Kilmallock, Limerick, Murroe, Newcastle West, Oola, Pallaskenry, Rathkeale, Shanagolden and Tournafulla. *Slater's Directory of Adare and Croom, Askeaton, Castle-connell and O'Brien's Bridge, Foynes, Kilmallock, Limerick, Newcastle West and Rathkeale* came out in 1870 and 1881. Limerick names can also be traced in *Guy's Postal directory of Munster 1886* and *1893* respectively. Finally Slater's appeared again in 1894. The *Cork and Munster Trade Directory* is also worth checking. There are copies held locally in the City Library for the years 1914, 15, 18, 24, 25, 27, 28, 29 and for some of the nineteen thirties

Along with these guides other publications can be crosschecked for name references. Taylor and Skinner's *Road Maps of Ireland*, published by the

THE IRISH GENEALOGIST

FERRAR'S LIMERICK DIRECTORY 1769[1]

FERRAR'S LIMERICK DIRECTORY
Containing
MERCHANTS, TRADERS, and others, etc.

Note. E stands for Englishtown, and I for Irishtown.

A

Alcock Nathaniel, Auctioneer, Peter's-street.
Allen Joseph, Hosier, Main-street, E.
Alley Thomas and Sons, Woollen-drapers.
    Main street, E.
Alley Thomas, Chandler, Main-street, E.
Alley William, Wine Merchant, Main-street, E.
Allison, James, Baker, Main-street, E.
Ambrose Stephen, Vintner, Quay Lane.
Anketile John, Wine Merchant, Main-street, E.
Arthur Patrick, Merchant, Main-street, I.
Arthur Joseph, Merchant, Main-street, I.
Atkinson, Henry, Rope maker, Pennywell.

B

Bagwell Thomas, Grocer, Parade.
Ball Joseph, Publican. Parade.
Bine Daniel, Smith, Shamble-lane.
Barry Michael, Woollen-draper, Main-street, E.
Barry James, Tobacconist, Baal's-bridge.
Barrington, Jane, Pewterer, Main-street, I.
Barton Nicholas, Brush-maker, Mungret-street.
Beauchamp Robert, Clothier, Thomond-gate.
Belt Peter,   } Card-makers, Baal's-bridge.
Belt George,   }
Bennis Richard, Innholder, Little Fish-lane.
Bennis Jacob, Peruke-maker, Main-street, E.
Bennis John, Smith, Mungret-street.
Barkery John, Grocer, John-street.
Barry Charles, Tinman, Baal's-bridge.
Blood Neptune, Salt-boiler, Thomond-gate.
Blood Charles, Tobacconist, Main-street, E.
Blood Jeremiah, Tobacconist, Baal's-bridge.
Bluett Patrick, Merchant, Main-street, E.
Bluett Catherine, Wine Merchant, Main-street,
    E.
Bluett Laurence, Taylor, Main-street. E.
Boulster Richard, Sadler, John-street.
Bourchier Thomas, Gunsmith, Main-street, E.
Bourke Patrick, Haberdasher, Main-street, E.
Bourke William, Wine Merchant, Main-street, E.
Bourke Miles, Sadler, Exchange.
Bourke John, Peruke-maker, John-street.
Bourke Margaret, Milliner, Parade.
Bourke Walter, Teacher of the Latin, Fish-lane.
Bowdy John, Woollen-draper, Mungret-street.
Bowen Henry, Master of Dr. Hall's School,
    Parade.
Boyle James, Publican, Main-street, E.

Boyle Patrick, Hosier, Main-street, E.
Brenan John, Brewer, John's-gate.
Brehon Thomas, Carpenter, Change-lane.
Bromwell Benjamin, Smith, John's-gate.
Brown James, Merchant, Main-street, E.
Brown Thomas, Grocer, Parade.
Browning Hercules, Linen-bleacher, Maia-
    street, E.
Brown William, Slater, Back-lane, Market-
    house.
Bruce Robert, Baker, John-street.
Brush George, Jeweller, Main-street, E.
Bryan John, Publican, Main-street, E.
Bull Abae, Grocer, Main-street, E.
Burrowes Thomas, Shoemaker, Main-street, E.
Bushell Benjamin, Chandler, Mungret-street.
Bushell Ralph, Chandler, John-street.
Byrne Thomas, Paper-stamper, John-street.
Byrun William, Carpenter, Market-house.
Byrun John, Carpenter, Main-street, E.

C

Caffry Margaret, Milliner, Main-street, E.
Callinan David, Woollen-draper, Main-street, I.
Canny William, Woollen-draper, Baal's Bridge.
Carr Robert, Tanner, Main-street, E.
Carr Thomas, Gunsmith, Main-street, E.
Carrige David, Brewer, Thomond-gate.
Carrol Anthony, Coach-maker, Mungret-street.
Carrol James, Grocer, Main-street, E.
Carter Mary, Haberdasher, Quay-lane.
Carthy Daniel, Fruiterer, Main-street, I.
Casey Thomas, Merchant, Old Quay.
Chamberlain Richard, Chandler, Main-street, E.
Chambers Robert, Chandler, Market-house.
Charlies Peter, French-master, Barrack-street.
Cherry John, Printer, Pery-street.
Conrell John, Brewer, John's-gate.
Counery Patrick, Cabinet-maker, John's-gate.
Conway Luke, Shoe-maker, Market-house.
Conyn Thomas, Tanner, John's-gate.
Clunchy Thomas, Tobacconist, John-street, I.
Clunchy Sarah, Grocer, Market-house.
Clohesy Derby, Linen-draper, Main-street, I.
Clowden James, Cooper, Peter's-cell.
Coles Christopher, Architect, Main-street, E.
Collins Michael, Cutler, Parade.
Connolly Patrick, Publican, Quay-lane.
Considine Daniel, Publican, Old Quay.

---

1. Only three copies are known to exist of this directory which appears to be the first ever printed
for Limerick.

A page from *Ferrar's Limerick Directory 1769*
- The Irish Genealogist 3 (9) 1964.

authors in Dublin and London in 1778 contains maps of the main roads of Ireland in the early 19th century, and shows the houses of the principal gentry. You should also look at *The Post Chaise Companion through Ireland*, Dublin 1805 (Eds. from 1783) 'with particulars of the noblemen and gentlemen's seats'.

While you may not be able to make a definite link with the names mentioned these directories can establish an early occurrence of a family name. This is true especially of the tradespeople. It is also wonderful to be able to link your name to an ancestor who was a saddler, haberdasher or teacher of Latin. However it is important to note that the majority of the population will not be listed. The directories tended to list the more prosperous members of society.

Most of these titles are held by the National Library of Ireland and by university libraries such as that of Trinity College Dublin and University College Cork (especially for Guy's directories). Limerick County Library holds-Ferrar's, Lucas', Pigot's 1824 and Bassett's 1880-81. They also hold Taylor and Skinner's *Road Maps of Ireland* and *The Post Chaise Companion*. The City Library holds all the above excepting Taylor and Skinner, plus Guy's *Munster Directory*, the *New Triennial Commercial Directory of 1840*, Slater's *Munster Directory of 1846*, and *Directory of Principal Towns for 1877/78* and a *Limerick City Directory for 1879*. This library also holds *The Limerick city and county of Limerick and Clare directory 1891-92*. As most of the above titles are out of print it would be well to do a check of the library catalogues available on the web in order to identify their location (see chapter 13). Holden's directory is on LDS film 100179 and 258722. Ferrar's Directory is published in *Ir. Gen.* 1964, 3, (9) p. 329-340 and Lucas' is in the *Ir.Gen.* 1967, 3, (12) p. 529-537. Note that Ferrar's of 1769 is on the internet at *http: //members.aol.com/LABATH/limerick.htm* and is on LDS film 941.5 A1 and Lucas' 1788 directory can also be accessed at http://members.aol.com/LABATH/lim1788.htm

O'Brien, family of:

Inchiquin Papers: Wills, administrations and marriage settlements of various members of the family of O'Brien, Earls of Thomond, and associates, 1551, 17 - 18th c. (Now in National Library of Ireland. For further particulars see The Inchiquin Mss., ed. by J. Ainsworth, 1961.)

O'Brien, family of:

Inchiquin Papers: About one thousand letters to or by members of the family of O'Brien, Earls of Thomond, on domestic, estate and other topics, a few 16th and early 17th c. mainly 1680 - early 19th c. (Now in National Library of Ireland. For further particulars see The Inchiquin Mss., ed. by J. Ainsworth, 1961.)

O'Brien, family of:

Inchiquin Papers: Bills, answers and other documents in legal cases involving members of the family of O'Brien, Earls of Thomond, and mainly concerning property in co. Clare, 1599 and 17th and 18th c. (Now in National Library of Ireland. For further particulars see The Inchiquin Mss., ed. by J. Ainsworth, 1961.)

O'Brien, family of:

Inchiquin Papers: Petitions and other documents concerning members of the family of O'Brien, Earls of Thomond, and others involved in the confederate and Williamite wars, mainly in cos. Clare and Kerry. (Now in National Library of Ireland. For further particulars see The Inchiquin Mss., ed. by J.F. Ainsworth, 1961.)

O'Brien, family of:

Inchiquin Papers: Pedigrees and letters on the genealogy of the families of O'Brien, Earls of Thomond, etc., Smith of Cahirmoyle, with associated documents. (Now in National Library of Ireland. For further particulars see The Inchiquin Mss., ed. by J.F. Ainsworth, 1961.)

O'Brien, family of:

O'Brien, family of:

Genealogical Office Ms.158, p.65: Arms of Rt. Hon. Donal, Lord Obrien, Baron of Ibreakan, Earl of Thomond, c.1613.

O'Brien, family of:

Genealogical Office Ms.158, p.250: List of Arms of 37 family surnames displayed as part of the O'Brien genealogy, 1614—1700.

O'Brien, family of:

Genealogical Office Ms.158, p.248: Continuation of O'Brien Pedigrees of Earls of Thomond and Inchiquin and Viscount Clare, 1614—1700.

O'Brien, family of:

Madrid: Archivo Historico Nacional: Caballeros de Calatrava: Exp. 980. Frens y Obriens de Zuniga (Antonio), 1638; Exp.994. Fuit y Burgo (Ricardo), 1673; Exp. 1046. Geraldin y Geraldin (Diego), 1647; Exp.1812. Obruin y Hill (Arturo de), 1696.

                                    n.3186   p.2806

O'Brien, family of:

Genealogical Office Ms.35, pp.26-7: Emblazon of Coat of Arms (with alternative) and banner of Obrian, Barons of Insecoine, c.1640.

O'Brien, family of:

Genealogical Office Ms.178, p.383: Pedigree of O'Brien of Dromoland, with descent from Catherine Hyde, sister of Lady Anne Hyde, mother of Anne, Queen of England, c.1660 — 1816.

O'Brien, family of:

Genealogical Office Ms.173, p.152: Pedigree of Earldom of Orkney and its descent in female line from family of Hamilton through O'Brien to Fitzmaurice, 1666 — 1832.

A page from Hayes' Manuscript Catalogue showing entries for family related manuscripts

Chapter 11   Family Histories

Family histories are of two types (a) those which review the origin and general history of a family i.e. all holders of a particular name and (b) detailed histories of specific families. In the first category are such works as O'Hart's *Irish Pedigrees* pub. Dublin, 1887 and Edward McLysaght's *Irish Families- their names, arms and origins (*Dublin, Allen Figgis, 1972) and associated titles. These works provide general information on the origins and history of Irish family names. They may also highlight prominent families of a particular name. However, they rarely provide specific information on individuals.

There are also a considerable number of detailed family histories about Limerick families. The more prominent families, particularly Anglo- Irish stock, figure strongly. Burke's *Irish Family Records*(London, Burke's Peerage, 1976) is a specific source in tracing such families. There are also family histories that study a particular branch or branches for example, the O'Briens of Thomond (see below), and there are also publications by family researchers who have traced their own particular family tree. The following is a list of such publications but note that many local history journals also carry family histories. *Sources for Irish Family History* by James G. Ryan (Flyleaf Press, Dublin, 2001) lists books and articles on all Irish families.
In this chapter the specific family sources are presented as (a) books and articles (b) pedigrees and (c) family papers.

11.1 Books and Articles

General publications on famous residents and natives of Limerick include: *Worthies of Thomond - a compendium of short lives of the most famous men and women of Limerick and Clare to the present day* edited by Robert Herbert (Limerick 1944), *A commentary on the nobility and gentry of Thomond circa 1567* (from the Carte Mss. no.55 in the Bodleian Library) in *Ir.Gen.* 1969,4, (2) p.65-73 and Michael O'Laughlin's book *Families of County Limerick, Ireland – from earliest times to the 20ᵗʰ century,* Kansas, 1997. O'Lochlain. Specific books and articles include:

Arthur: 'The Arthur manuscript' by John Ainsworth, NMAJ 1957, 7 (4) p.4 -10 and 1959 8 (1) p.2-19
Aylmer: *The Aylmers of Ireland* by Sir Fenton Aylmer, London 1931.
Barrington: *The Barringtons: a family history* by Amy Barrington Dublin, 1917 see also OLJ vol. 24 (1988), the Barrington edition.
Bateman: *The Batemans of Ballymacreese* by Fr. Paul Bateman (Canberra 1985).

Bennis: *Some reminiscences of Limerick friends* by Ernest H. Bennis pub. Limerick, 1930 and OLJ 1999, 36 p. 55-60

Bevan: 'Bevan of Co. Limerick' *Ir. Anc.* 1974, p. 1-5

Blackall: 'Abstracts from Blackall family records' by Hon. H.W.B. Blackall *Ir. Gen.* 1941 1 (9) p.265-272

Blennerhassett: Blennerhassett of Riddlestown and Rockfield, Co. Limerick in *Selections from Old Kerry Records* by Mary Agnes Hickson, London 1872 and see also Burke's *Irish Family Records* p. 133-142 (see paragraph above)

Bourke: 'The Bourkes of Clanwilliam' by James Grene Barry in JRHAAI 1889, 9, p. 192-201.

Brassil: The Brassils of Co.Kerry, Clare and Limerick at http://www.iol.iegerardb/kerry.htm

Brien: See under O'Brien

Brown: *The Kenmare Manuscripts* by Edward McLysaght Dublin, 1942 covers the Brown family who had estates in Limerick.

Browne-de Burgh: *Notes on the history of the de Burgh family* by Elizabeth Jane Hussey de Burgh Dublin, 1890

Casey & Gallahue: 'Visit to the ancestral home at Gerah' by Valda Harmn in *Kilbehenny/Anglesboro Journal* 1990 p. 58-60

Colles: see ms. 544 GO records of the family of Colles and the Cook diary.

Connor: see under O'Connor

Croker: 'The family of Croker' in *Burke's Irish Family Records*, p. 295-297

Curling: 'The Curling Family –agents to the Devon estate Co.Limerick 1848-1943' by John Cussen in *Jnl.Newcastlewest Historical Society* 1990, 1, p.32-35

Curtin: *West Limerick roots- the Lawrence Curtin family of Knockbrack, Co. Limerick* by Paul J. Curtin(Austin, Texas 1995).

De Salis: see *Burke's Irish Family Records* p. 1009-1011

Desmond: 'Descendants of the last Earls of Desmond' by John O'Donovan in UJA 1858, 6.
As wicked a woman –the biography of Eleanor Countess of Desmond 1545-1638 by Anne Chambers (Dublin, Wolfhound Press, 1986).

De Valera: *De Valera and Bruree* by Mainchin Seoighe published by De Valera Museum Bruree 1985

D'Esterre: 'D'Esterre of Rossmanagher' by Esme F.H. Colley (has many references to Limerick) in the *Ir. Gen.* 1979 5 (6) p. 720-727

Drew: *The Drews of Dromlohan – a preliminary history of the Drew family from Dromlohan Townland, Kilcornan parish, county Limerick* by Carol Baxter(St. Ives, NSW 1996).

Dundon: *More Dundons – the Dundons of county Limerick* by John Dundon pub. Dun Laoghaire Co. Dublin by John Dundon. Copy in NLI.

Dunraven: (Wyndham-Quin) *Memorials of Adare* by Caroline Countess of Dunraven. Oxford, private circulation, 1865.

Fennell: *The Fennells of Manister, Co.Limerick* by Paul D. Fennell, Orlando, Florida, Paul Fenell, 2000

Ferrar: see Huntingdon

FitzGerald: 'The Four Brothers-eighteenth century knights of Glin' by T.H. Byrne in *The Glencorbry Chronicle* 2001 1 (2) p. 28-48; *The Knights of Glin -a Geraldine family* by J. Anthony Gaughan, Dublin, Kingdom Books 1978; *The Fitzgerald Geraldines Earls of Desmond* by Rev. C.P. Meehan, Dublin 1852; 'The Geraldines of Desmond' from Michael O'Clery's book of pedigrees edited by Canon Hayman in JRSAI 1880-81, 25 and 1885, 17, p. 211 ff; *In Veronica's garden* by Margaret Cadwalader pub. Qualicum, British Colombia Madrona Books 2003 [deals with FitzGerald family of Glin castle]

FitzGibbon: 'Unpublished Geraldine documents' edited by Canon Samuel Hayman JRHAAI 1876-78, 4 (4) p. 14-52 and p. 299-355 [pedigree of FitzGibbons including FitzGibbon of Knocklong and O'Grady of Kilballyowen].

Gabbett: *Lineage of the Gabbett family of Caherline, County Limerick.* Printed for private circulation, Limerick, n.d.

Gallahue: 'The Gallahues of Anglesboro' by Liam Coughlan in KA 1989, 17 p. 33-35,

Gallivan: *The Gallivans of Limerick - genealogy* by G.P. Gallivan pub. Glenageary Co. Dublin 1995 by the author. Copy in NLI.

Galvin: Galvin family of Lackendarra. KA 1995-96 p. 59-64

Galwey: 'The Galweys of Munster' by Sir Henry Blackall reprinted from JCHAS 1966, 71 p. 138-158 and 1967 72 p. 20-47 and 1968 73 p. 161-173 [includes Limerick Galweys]

Goold: The Goold family, Athea, Co.Limerick in *The Dublin Builder* 1863.

Gough: *The life and campaigns of Hugh first Viscount Gough Field-Marshal* by Robert S. Rait pub. Westminster, Archibald Constable, 1903.[Gough of Woodsdown, Co. Limerick]

Grady: see O'Grady

Griffin: 'Limerick and Gerald Griffin with a pedigree of the Griffin family' by Rev. Patrick Moloney in NMAJ 1940-4, 2 (1) p. 4-13

Gubbins: 'The Gubbins Family' by Michael F. O'Sullivan in LGDJ, 1996, no. 9 p. 20-23

Harding: see *From Bruree to Corcomohide* by Mainchin Seoighe, Limerick, 2000.

Harte: 'Harte of Co. Limerick' pedigree in *Swanzy Notebooks*, vol. 22 p. 720, RCBL, Dublin.

Hayes: *Ossianic and other verse in Irish with notes on the family of Hayes of Caherguillamore Co.Limerick* 1843 NLI ms.8 (Hogan); *The descendants of Patrick Hayes* by Nitko V. Vail and Shiela Delaney Heffernan [unpub] a Doon family - copy in Limerick City Library.

Hewetson/ Hewson: *Memoirs of the house of Hewetson or Hewson of Ireland* by John Hewetson, London, Mitchell and Hughes, 1901.

Hickey: *A little of Limerick – an account of the Hickey, Scanlan and Baggott families of Campedown and Cobden* by J. & S. Walter, Australia, 1999 [roots in Caherconlish area] 'The O'Hickeys-hereditary physicians to the O'Briens of Thomond and some of their descendants' by Lieut.Col. J. Hickey NMAJ 1958 8 (1) p. 38-41.

Hodges: 'The family of Hodges and Morgan of Old Abbey , Co. Limerick' by M. J. Dore in *Ir. Anc.* 1979, 11 (2) p. 77-84

Hogan: *The quest for the galloping Hogan* by Matthew J.Culligan-Hogan, New York, Crown Publications. 1979

Howard: *To hell or to Hobart* by Patrick Howard pub. NSW, Kangaroo Press, 1993.

Hunt: *The Hunt family of Ireland* by Fred J.R. Hunt. This is a microfilm copy, which contains records of Hunts and deeds of descendants of Captain Vere Hunt of Limerick and Tipperary 1731-1931- LDS film 1364336 items 9-11. Transcript held by the Genealogical Society of Victoria, Australia.

Huntingdon /Ferrar: *The Limerick Huntingdon Ferrars by one of them* (Michael Lloyd Ferrar) Plymouth, England, 1903

Hurley: see O'Hurley

Lacy: *The Roll of the House of Lacy* by De Lacy –Bellingari, Baltimore, 1928. 'The de Lacy family of Bruff' by Prof. Daithi O hOgain in *The Dawn* 1996 p. 3-8

Langford: 'The Langfords of Kilcosgriff, Co.Limerick' listed in *Bibliography of Irish Family History and Genealogy* by Brian de Breffny and see also *Ir. Anc.* 1985, 17 (1) p. 18-23

Langton: see *From Bruree to Corcomohide* by Mainchin Seoighe, Limerick 2000.

Le Fanu: see *Burke's Irish Family Records* p. 705-708

Loftus: 'Loftus family in Mungret' by Rev. Michael Moloney in NMAJ 1944, 4 (1) p. 11-15

McEniry: see *From Bruree to Corcomohide* by Mainchin Seoighe, Limerick 2002.

MacLysaght: *The name MacLysaght /Lysaght and its origins* by William McLysaght, Limerick, Treaty Press 1979

MacSheehys: 'The MacSheehys of Connello in Co.Limerick' by Hubert Gallwey in *Ir.Gen.* 1973, 4, (6) p. 564-577

MacSweeney: *Leabhar Chlainne Suibhne –an account of the MacSweeney families in Ireland with pedigree* by Rev. Paul Walsh Dublin, 1920

McMahons: 'The French McMahons' by Denis McMahon in OLJ (French edition) 1989, 25 p. 105-112.

Mahony: 'A family of Mahony in counties Kerry and Limerick' by Brian de Breffny *Ir. Anc.* 13 (1) p. 1-3

Massy: Anon , *A genealogical account of the Massey family from the time of the conquest.* Dublin, 1890. See also *Burke's Irish Family Records* p. 788-792, *The abduction of a Limerick heiress* by Toby Barnard, Maynooth [Studies in local history series] 1998 [Massy heiress 18th C.]

Maunsell: *History of the Maunsell family* by R.G. Maunsell Cork, 1903

Millers: *All worlds possible –the domain of the Millers of Coolybrown* by

P.J.O'Connor, Oireacht na Mumhan, 1993

Moloney: 'The Moloneys of Kiltanon' by Kevin Hannan in OLJ 1989, 25, p.11-13.

Monckton: 'Monckton of Co. Limerick' *Ir. Anc.* 1972, p. 15-21

Monsell: *The life and times of William Monsell, 1ˢᵗ Baron of Tervoe (1812-1894) by Matthew Potter,* Limerick, 1995.

Moore: Moores of North Kerry and West Limerick by Martin Moore in *Ballyguiltenane Rural Journal* 1998/99, p.64-65 part 1, part 2 ibid 1999/2000 p.43-44.

Nihell: 'Nihell of Counties Clare and Limerick' by James M. Niall in *Ir.Gen.* 1972, 4, (5) p.496 - 506.

Nunan: *The Nunans of the province of Munster, Ireland* by Francis Nunan Howard pub. New York 1970 by the author

O'Brien: 'The O'Brien Sept' by Sean Murphy in *Ir. Roots* 1996 no.1 p. 17; 'Carrigogunnell Castle and the O'Briens of Pubblebrien in the Co. of Limerick' by T.J. Westropp JRSAI 1907 37, p. 374-392 and 38 (1908) p. 141-160 and 40 (1910) p. 38 ff.

History of the O'Briens by Hon. Donough O'Brien London, Batsford 1949
These my friends and forbears- the O'Briens of Dromoland by Grania R. O'Brien Whitegate, Co.Clare, Ballinakella Press.

History of the name O'Brien by J.D. Williams, Cork: Mercier Press, 1977. 'The O'Briens in Munster after Clontarf'by the Rev. John Ryan in the NMAJ 1941, 2 (4) p. 141-152 and 3 (1) 1942 p. 1-52.

The O'Briens in Irish history 1500-1865 by Ivar O'Brien, Sussex, England, Phillimore, 1986.

There is an extensive web site for the O'Brien clan at www.obrienclann.com

O'Connor: 'The O'Connor septs' by Sean Murphy in *Irish Roots* 1995 no.2 p. 16.

Odell: 'The Family of Odell or O'Dell' by Brian de Breffny in *Ir. Anc.* 1969, 1 (2) and 1971, 3 (1) p. 41-48.

O'Daly: 'The O'Daly- poets of Corcomroe' by Eilis Ni Mhurcadha in NMAJ 1940, 1 (2) p.35-36

O'Grady: 'O'Grady of Capercullen' by L .J. Bardwick NMAJ 1957, 7 (4) p. 20-22; 'The O'Grady connection' in *Rambling through Knockaney* published by Knockaney G.A.A.; 'O'Grady of Kilballyowen Co. Limerick' in *An. Hib.* 15 p. 35-62.

O'Hurley: 'Some account of the family of O'Hurly' in JCHAS, 1905, 11, p.105-23 and p.177-83, also 1906, 12, p26-33 and 76-88.

O'Ryan: *Four Tipperary Septs* by Martin Callanan Galway, O'Gorman, 1938 for a comprehensive account of the O'Mulryans.

O'Shaughnessy: *The O'Shaughnessys of Munster –the people and their stories* by John M. Feheney, Cork Iverus Publications,1996.'Limerick O'Shaughnessys' by John M. Feheney in *Ir. Fam.Hist* 1993, 9 p.10-16.

O'Toomey: *The O'Toomeys of Croom and their descendants by Thomas*

Noxon Toomey, private distribution, Saint-Louis, Miss. 1920.

Pennefeather, Penefather: *4 typed volumes of family records* by Rev.James Pennefeather, Lisnagry, Co.Limerick 1966 (held by Soc. of Genealogists, London).

Peppard: 'The Peppards of Cappagh, Co. Limerick' by Brian de Breffny *Ir. Anc.* 1984, 16 (2) p. 68-70

Purcell: see JRSAI 1903, 33 p. 167-169 and p. 171

Ranahan: *The Ranahans of Iverus-history and directory* by John P.M. Feheney, Cork, Iverus Publications, 1987

Roche: 'Roches of Newcastlewest, Co. Limerick' *Ir. Gen.* 1950, p. 244-245

Russell: 'The Russells of Limerick' by Hampden William Russell in NMAJ 1950, 6 (2) p. 50-51.

Ryan: 'From the rocks of Limerick to the rocks of Sydney' by Christopher Ryan in *Ir.Fam.Hist.* 1992, 1, (8) p. 16-20; 'The Ryans of Temple Mungret – four generations of the family' in the *Limerick Leader* newspaper June 9, 1945; *My privileged life – at Scarteen with the Black and Tans* by Thady Ryan. Derrydale Press, Lanham, MD published 2002. [Ryan family Knocklong]; *Ryan O'Maoilriain* by Daithi O hOgain, Dublin, Gill & Macmillan, 2003.

Scanlan: 'Scanlan of Connello Barony, Co.Limerick' by Brien de Breffny and A. E. Evers in the *Ir. Anc* .1972, 4, (2) p. 71-80.

Shaughnessy: *The O'Shaughnessys of Munster – the people and their stories* by John P. M. Feheny, Blarney, Co. Cork, 1996.

Sullivan: *The James Sullivan family – emigrants from Lisready Cripps, Loughill, county Limerick and their descendants* by Rita J. Meistrell(pub. Los Angeles by the author in 1999).

de Stacpoole: see Burkes *Landed Gentry 1958*; *History of the Stacpoole family of counties Clare and Limerick 1596-1959* by R.J.Stacpoole in the NLI; *Stacpoole –the owners of a name* by John Stacpoole, 1991 (limited edition, Auckland).

Stephenson: 'The Stephensons – sixty years of Limerick history' by Thomas Pierce in *North Munster Studies* edited by Etienne Rynne pub. Limerick, Thomond Archaeological Society 1967.

Tuthill: *Pedigree of the family of Tuthill and Villiers of Co. Limerick* by P.B. Tuthill, London, 1908.

Vereker: 'The Vereker family' by Brian de Breffny. *Ir. Anc.* 1973, 5 (2) p. 69-75

Villiers: *Pedigree of the family of Villiers of Kilpeacon, Co. Limerick* by P.B. Tuthill, London,   1907.

Vincent: 'The Vincent family of Limerick and Clare' by Berkeley L. Vincent. *Ir.Gen.* 1971, 4 (4) p. 342-348.

Wall: *The Wall family in Ireland* by Hubert Gallwey 1970.

Warter: *The Warter family in Bilboa Co. Limerick 1640-1830* by Veronica Walsh Irish Times project for young county historian 1990-91 (held in the County Library).

Westropp: *The Westropp family 1250-2000* by G. Westropp and H. Elliott

Cooper, London, 1999.
White: *The history of the family of White of Limerick* by John D.White, Cashel, Co. Tipperary, 1887 (held in NLI).

11.2 Pedigrees

There are numerous pedigrees of Limerick families in various archives, particularly the Genealogical Office (See chapter 13). Note however, that a pedigree will generally only define the lineal descent from one ancestor. It will not provide information on all persons with a particular family name. The principal pedigrees relating to Limerick are given below. For the sake of simplicity only the GO manuscript numbers and the references to the family name in Limerick are given. References to other scions of the families in other parts of the country have been excluded. To see the full pedigree, refer to Hayes' *Manuscript Sources vol. 8 Places.*

Ms. 806: draft pedigree of the Arthur families of Dublin and Limerick
          c.1600-1740.
Ms. 93: pedigree of Ashe of Croagh and Glynn Co.Limerick
Ms. 178: pedigree of Bagot of Ballinstown and Rathjordan
Ms. 180: pedigree of Barry of Ballyguybeg and Bohergar and Farnane,
          Rochestown and Fryarstown now Sandville all in Co. Limerick
          c.1570-1892
Ms. N4216: Blennerhassett of Riddlestown
Ms. 159: of Bourke of Ballyvorneen of Ballycharra, Dromkeen and
          Newcastle with mention of Ballynaguard Co.Limerick
Ms. 159: of Browne of Hospital Co.Limerick c.1550-1640
Ms. 176: of de Burgh of Dromkeen Co.Limerick and see also ms.169 Bourk
          of Castleconnell and Dromkeen 814-1845
Ms. 171: of Compton of Glynn Co.Limerick
Ms. 107: Coopers of Cooper Hill
Ms. 173: of Coote of Mount Coote Co.Limerick
Ms. 520: pedigrees of Counties Clare, Galway and Limerick families. Also
          LDS British film 257821 item 7.
Ms. 171: of Delmage of Rathkeale and also copy of confirmation of arms
          for Delmage.
Ms. 108: Dickson of Ballynguile and Clounleharde county Limerick
Ms. 178: of Evans of Ballygrenane, of Caherass and Bulgaden Hall, of
          Fanningstown ....of Ash Hill Tower and Bushy Island.
Ms. 175: of Finch of the Abbey Co.Limerick c.1544-1842
Ms. 168: of Fitzgerald...c.1100-1824 see also ms.112
Ms. 168: of Fitzgerald of Ballynard, Ballyrobin and of Bellfield Co.Limerick
          and see also ms.112
Ms. 171: of Fitzgerald Knight of Glynn c.1275-1937
Ms. 180: of Fitzgibbon, mac an tSen Riddery, the White Knight...

Ms. 164: of Franklin of Portrane Co.Limerick

Ms. 178: of Greene of Ballymacreese

Ms. 164: of Harrold of Limerick c.1650-1720 and ms.177 c.1650-1783

Ms. 804(3): draft pedigree of Hawkins of Rathkeale

Ms. 176: of Hayes of Caherguillamore Co.Limerick c.1730-1800

Ms. 165 & 174: of Herbert of Rathkeale c.1550-1781

Ms. 805: of Hunt of Inchirourke Co. Limerick

Ms. 180: of Hunt Curragh Chase Co.Limerick

Ms. 108: note on the descent of Sir Thomas Hurley Baronet of Knocklong

Ms. 811(32): draft pedigree of Keating of Baybush Co.Limerick c.1400-1780

Ms. 810: draft pedigree of Kiggell of Cahara and Birchwood both of Glin and
          Camas Newcastle-West Co.Limerick 1742-1913

Ms. 810: of miscellaneous information about Keyes and Keays family of
          Newcastle West and Knocklong c.1620-1900

Ms. 176: of de Lacy ....of Athlacca, of Rathcahill, of Templeglanton of
          Ballylaghen of Dromada all in Co. Limerick and also see ms.177

Ms. 142: pedigree of Lloyd of Newtown Pery Co.Limerick 1785-96

Ms. 175: of Macgillysacht also Lysaght/McLysaght of Tullybrack &
          Camas in Co.Limerick

Ms. 113: of McMahon of Limerick c.1750-1815

Ms. 112: of Massey of Duntrileague ...and of New Garden, Stoneville

Ms. 164: of Meade of Kilmallock c1660-1770

Ms. 178: of Minnitt of Mount Minnitt Co.Limerick

Ms. 816(16): of Morgan of Old Abbey Co.Limerick 1598-1937

Ms. 161: of Moroney of Faningstown c1600-1700

Ms. 171: of Maunsell of Caherdavin Co.Limerick 1577-1940

Ms. 160: of Nihell 777AD-1723

Ms. 178: of O'Brien, Earls and Barons Inchiquin and of Cahermoyle
          Co.Limerick c.1206-1855; also Ms.158 Donal O'Brien Earl of
          Thomond and Brien of Carriggogonnell; Ms. 179: of O'Brien of the
          city of Limerick c.1730-1855.

Ms. 162: of O'Connell of Castleconnell Co.Limerick c1300-1755

Ms. 169: of Odell of Palace, of Ballingarry , of Shannon Grove...

Ms. 182: of O'Donnell of Limerick

Ms. 176: of O'Grady of Caherguillamore: see also ms.164 O'Grady of
          Killballyowen

Ms. 173: of O'Halloran of Limerick c.1750-1835

Ms. 168: of Oliver Kilfinane and Castle Oliver Co.Limerick c.1650-1810

Ms. 177: of O'Mahony (with Limerick references).

Ms. 13,066: of Peppard mainly of Limerick

Ms. 814: of Peacocke of Fort Etna Co.Limerick

Ms. 180: of Pigot of Kilfinny and Rathkeale Co.Limerick

Ms. 94: of Quin of Adare, Earls of Dunraven 1709-1838 also ms. 94
            c.(1600-1800); ms.168 (c.1600-1810); ms.178 (c.1645-1796)

Ms. 107: Rice and Spring Rice of Cappagh

Ms. 112: Roche of Newcastle and of Carrass; See also Ir.Gen. vol. 2 no 8 re:
Sir Boyle Roche, Bart by T. Blake Butler

Ms. 174: Rose of Morgans and Mount Pleasant and of Aghabeg & Rathkeal
Co.Limerick

Ms. 171: of Ryves of Caherconlish Co.Limerick

Ms. 202: (Gilbert collection Dublin City Library) pedigrees relating to the
Sarsfield family of Cork and Limerick, also ms.159 Sarsfield
of Kilmallock c.1400-1700

Ms. 169: pedigree of Sexton c.1480-1680

Ms. 112: of Smyth of Limerick

Ms. 112: of Southwell of Singland and Castlemattress(Castlematrix) and
Danesfort Co.Limerick c.1480-1810 and see also ms.160

Ms. 176: of Taylor of Ballynort and Barton in Co.Limerick

Ms. 159: of Terry of Kilmallock Co.Limerick c.1600-1700

Ms. 112: of Tierney of Ballyscandland Co.Limerick

Ms. 177: of Toomey and O'Toomey of Croom, Bruree and Newcastle West
Co.Limerick

Ms. 163: of Turner of Limerick city c.1459-1688

Ms. 171: of Vandeleur of Ballynamona Co.Limerick

Ms. 112: of Veracre afterwards Vereker of Grange in the south Liberties of
Co.Limerick

Ms. 111 &180: Verschoyle of Athea

Ms. 173: of Villiers Kilpeacon c.1670-1783

Ms. 162: of Wall of Dunmoylan Co.Limerick

Ms. 179: of Waller of the city of Limerick

Ms. 164: of Waters of Newcastle Co.Limerick c.1680-1786

Ms. 180: of Westropp....of Limerick city and Attyflin and Ballysteen

Ms. 159: of White of Rathgoonan Co.Limerick

Ms. 179: of Wilson, city of Limerick, Caherconlish & Bilbo Co. Limerick
c.1620-1849

The LDS Family History Catalogue lists the Molony pedigrees. This film is a
copy of manuscripts held in the GO. Among other things it lists ms.452 - Vital
records extracted from the *General Advertiser and Limerick Gazette* for the
period 1804-1879. It also lists ms.455 Vital records extracted from the *Clare
Journal* and the *Limerick Gazette and Chronicle* 1778-1854.

The GO also has confirmations and grants of arms documents that confirm
the right to bear arms by certain families. The right to claim arms must be
confirmed by proof of descent from a member of the family whose right to the
arms was recorded in the Genealogical Office.

Ms. 107: copy of confirmation of arms to Joseph Barrington of the city of
Limerick 1831

Ms. 111: confirmation of arms to the descendants of James Barry of

Fryarstown, now Sandville, Co.Limerick

Ms. 108: copy of confirmation to arms to Isaac Butt M.P. grandson of Isaac
    Butt, Adare

Ms. 107: copy of confirmation of arms to the descendants of Robert Cox,
    who was granted the lands of Ballynoe and Ballyscanlon in
    Co.Limerick in 1637 and to his descendant Wm. Cox April 1839

Ms. 107: to Adam Delmege late of Rathkeale, Co.Limerick

Ms. 108: to the descendants of Samuel Dickson of Ballynaguile

Ms. 111: to Patrick Donelan of Mount Kennett Co.Limerick

Ms. 111: to the descendants of William Hugh Ferrar son of John Ferrar
    Sheriff of Limerick

Ms. 107: to Sir Richard Frenklin 1841

Ms. 108: to the descendants of Thomas Franks and to his grandson John
    Franks of Ballyscaddane Castle, Co.Limerick

Ms. 108: to the descendants of John Goold and his wife Mary Quin of
    Rosbrien, Co.Limerick.

Ms. 109: to the descendants of John Crosbie Graves, grandson of James
    Graves Rector of Croom and Adare

Ms. 111a: copy of confirmation of arms to the descendants of Joseph
        Gubbins....

Ms. 112: arms of Vere Hunt, Curragh Chase, Co.Limerick

Ms. 111q: copy of confirmation of arms to Capt.Richard Kane of Limerick

Ms. 111b: of Francis Kearney of the city of Limerick

Ms. 111f: to the descendants of Wm.Langford of Gurteengary, Co.Limerick

Ms. 109: copy of grant of arms to the descendants of James Lenihan of
    Waterford and to Maurice Lenihan M.R.I.A. 1871

Ms. 105: to the descendants of Simon Low of Galbally Co.Limerick

Ms. 111: to the descendants of James Denis Lyons of Croom House

Ms. 106: to the descendants of John McMahon patentee comptroller of the
    port of Limerick

Ms. 108: to the descendants of John McMurray of Roxborough House

Ms. 105: to John Fitzgerald Magrath of Bellfield, on North Strand, City of
    Limerick

Ms. 150: copy of royal licence to Wm. Fitzgerald Magrath, late of Bellfield..

Ms. 109: copy of grant of arms to Rev.John Maunsell Massy of Barna

Ms. 111g: grant of arms to Mark Frederick Wyndham Maunsell of
        Finneterstown, Adare

Ms. 110: copy of confirmation of arms to the descendants of James O'Brien

Ms. 111h: folio 88 to the descendants of Benjamin O'Donovan

Ms. 111a: p.46 to O'Grady

Ms. 105: to the descendants of Robert Oliver of Clonodfoy, also ms.168

Ms. 111: confirmation of arms to the descendants of Richard Plummer

Ms. 111b: folio 55, descendants of James Quin of Glenquin Castle

Ms. 104: arms entry of Thady Quin of Adare J.P. 1688 and see also ms.108

Ms. 107: grant of arms to descendants of David Roche late of Carass

Ms. 107: confirmation of arms to Wellington Anderson Rose of Foxhall,
    Co.Tipperary with an account of his descent from Rose of Morgans,
    Co.Limerick
Ms. 111: to the descendants of William Theobald Russell
Ms. 11f : folio 155 …to Thaddeus Richard Ryan and to his son John Joseph
    Ryan of Scarteen, Knocklong 1938
Ms. 111a: to the descendants of the Rev.John Crossley Seymour, Vicar of
    Caherelly.
Ms. 109: to Peter Tait of South Hill 1868
Ms. 103: arms entry of Michael Tierney of Limerick c.1749
Ms. 111c: to the descendants of Daniel McThomas Toomey of Newcastle
    West.

11.3 Family Papers

The **NAI** has the following:

Ms. 8993: Brown papers relating to the estates of the Brown and the related
    families of Pearse, Westropp and Rolleston 18th and 19th centuries,
    see McLysaght in *An. Hib.* No.15 1944
Ms. 5992: Papers relating to the Levers family of Counties Clare & Limerick
    1669-1870
Ms.   488: papers relating to the Dwyer family of Co. Limerick 1670-1809;
    papers relating to the Pearce or Pearse family of Co.Limerick
    early18th. century.
Ms. 85,90: notes relating to Scull & Seymour families of Co.Limerick
Ms. 5825(1-51): papers relating to the property of the Tuthill family (name
    changed to Villiers of one branch) especially Ballyteigue
d18156-64: papers relating to the Woodcock family of Rathkeale 1792-1827

The **NLI** has the following papers-

Ms. 8473: Bourke papers, Bourke family of Dromsally Co.Limerick
Ms.8998:   Brown papers – pedigree of the Brown family of Clare and
    Limerick
Ms .8384: documents relating to the family of Darcy Evans. Also documents
    relating to the Felan family, and the family of Greene 1732-1872
Ainsworth J.F.: Report on the Fitzgerald Papers (from 1744) held in Limerick
    City Library
Ms. 7976: Gilbourne family of Co. Limerick and allied families
Ms. 8482: papers, letters and estate accounts relating to the Oliver family of
    Castle Oliver Co. Limerick 1811-1828
Ms. 13,066: tabular pedigree of the family of Peppard, mainly of Limerick;
    the Stacpoole family 1596-1959 ref. n5491 p5658
Report on the Oliver papers relating to the Oliver and Silver families of Castle

Oliver, Co. Limerick by J.F.Ainsworth
Harrold-Barry papers (from 1700) see McLysaght in *An. Hib.* No.15 1944
McLysaght papers relating to the families of Lysaght, McLysaght, Arthur,
Browne and Reddan see in *An. Hib.* No.15 1944
The Gabbett family-notes made by the Rev. R.J. Gabbett, rector of Shanagolden
Co. Limerick c.1860-70 NLI n3263 p2881
Vere Hunt papers in the Limerick City Archives see McLysaght in *An.
Hib.No.15 1944*
Report on the Wolfe papers ....relating to the Wolfe family and to lands in Co.
Kildare Offaly and Limerick (Ainsworth J.F.).

Miscellaneous Papers – held elsewhere

The Dunraven papers are held by the **PRONI** and comprise c. 1500 documents
and c. 225 volumes from 1574 and 1614-1930's deriving from the Wyndham-
Quin family of Adare manor. A complete description is given by APW
Malcomson on the PRONI website (see Chapter 13).
The PRONI also holds some papers relating to the FitzGeralds of Limerick. .
The **University of Limerick** holds the family papers of the FitzGeralds of Glin
Castle Co. Limerick.

The **Royal Irish Academy** has ms.23c 21(672), genealogies in the Irish
language of the Barrys, Fitzgeralds and Butlers by Eoghan Caomhanach of
Hospital Co.Limerick 1816-17.
Limerick City Library has a photostat of Additional Pery Papers (1719-1806)
that are held in the PRONI.

Worcester Record Office, England has ms.705 24/1802 letters and other
papers relating to estates in Co.Limerick of the Balfe family 1854-67.

Chapter 12   Further Reading & Useful Sources

12.1 General Publications

'A Bibliography of Limerick history and antiquities' by Roisin de Nais, Limerick; Treaty Press, 1962 although somewhat dated, this is still an excellent guide to published items and their location.

'A Guide to Local History Source Material held in Limerick County Library' by Margaret Franklin, updates this bibliography to the mid-eighties and is available in the Limerick County Library.

'A Topographical Dictionary of Ireland' by Samuel Lewis is extremely useful as it provides a brief history and economic and social outline for each civil parish and large town in 1837. This book also records the corresponding Catholic parish and the locations of Presbyterian congregations. First published in 1837 it has been republished by several publishers and is also available on the web at *www.lcc.ie*

'Bibliography of Irish Family History and Genealogy' by Brian de Breffny, Dublin, Golden Eagle Books, 1974 gives an excellent listing of family histories.   This has been updated in *'Sources for Irish Family History'* by James G Ryan (Dublin, Flyleaf Press 2001).

For further **guides to Irish Family History**, take a look at:
'Guide to Tracing Your Irish Ancestors' by John Grenham, Dublin Gill and Macmillan 1992, 2nd edition 1999.
'Irish Genealogy- A Record Finder' by D.F. Begley, Dublin, Heraldic Artists, 1987.
'Irish Records – Sources for family & Local History'. James G. Ryan. Ancestry Inc. Utah 1997
'Tracing Irish Ancestors' by Maire MacConghail and Paul Gorry, London, Robert Books 2000.

There are also a few general interest works which give accounts of significant periods in **Irish history**.

'The Munster Plantation –English migration to southern Ireland 1583-1641' by Michael MacCarthy-Morrogh, Oxford, Clarendon Press, 1986 covers the most significant period when new names became established in Munster and Limerick. See also ' The Cromwellian Settlement of the County of Limerick'

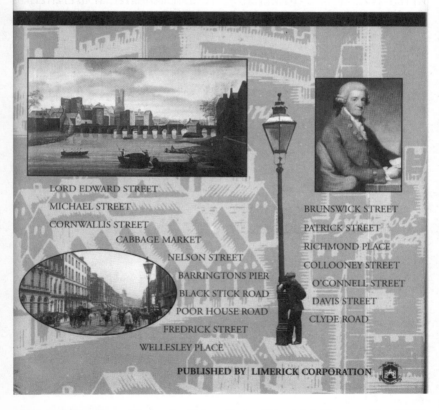

LIMERICK CITY
Street Names
GERRY JOYCE

LORD EDWARD STREET
MICHAEL STREET
CORNWALLIS STREET
CABBAGE MARKET
NELSON STREET
BARRINGTONS PIER
BLACK STICK ROAD
POOR HOUSE ROAD
FREDRICK STREET
WELLESLEY PLACE

BRUNSWICK STREET
PATRICK STREET
RICHMOND PLACE
COLLOONEY STREET
O'CONNELL STREET
DAVIS STREET
CLYDE ROAD

PUBLISHED BY LIMERICK CORPORATION

Limerick City Street Names by Gerry Joyce (Limerick Corporation 1995) provides a brief history of each street name, notes on place names and English to Irish translations.

by James Grene Barry in the *Limerick Field Club Journal* from 1900-1908. Barry's articles were effectively a serialised edition of the Books of Survey and Distribution (see chapter 3).

Readers are also recommended to consult some books dealing with the **Great Famine** (1845-47), as this was a major period of emigration and land ownership changes.

The Famine decade –contemporary accounts 1841-1851 ed. by John Killen Belfast, Blackstaff 1995 documents the period that was to see the major emigration of Irish to England, the U.S. and Australia. One can get a feel for the tremendous hardships endured by Irish families.

'*The Great Calamity-the Irish famine 1845-52*' by Christine Kinealy Dublin, Gill and MacMillan 1994 for another useful account of this period.

'*A Pauper Warren*' by Gerard Curtin deals specifically with the famine in West Limerick during the period 1845-49 (Sliabh Luachra Books 2000). *'Home Thoughts from Abroad'* by Thomas F. Culhane, Glin Historical Society 1998 gives a wonderful insight into emigrant life in Australia as well as of Glin and Limerick.

12.2   Publications of Limerick Interest

The following are useful accounts of various towns and parishes in Limerick. Over the last 10 years or so there has been a tremendous increase in publications of historical interest. Bookshops at home and abroad can supply all the major in-print publications quite easily. However sometimes the smaller locally-published histories can be difficult to find as copies may not given to the National Library which is a library of legal deposit. These smaller works are often well worth tracking down as they can often hold articles on the smaller local families and are often illustrated with old photographs that are quite appealing.

Adare:	'Adare and its poets' by Mainchin Seoighe in *The Capuchin Annual* 1964 p. 322-333
Ardpatrick:	*Ardpatrick –reflections historical & topographical on Ardpatrick Co. Limerick* by John Fleming
Askeaton:	'Notes on Askeaton' by T.J.Westropp in JRSAI 1904, Part 4 p. 111-132, and also *Eas Cead Tine Askeaton -800 years of history* by Patrick J.Cronin, Limerick; Askeaton Civic Trust 1999
Ballingarry:	*Records of Ballingarry* by Rev. G.F. Hamilton, (McKern and Sons, Limerick 1930) also *Ballingarry, Granagh and Clouncagh archival records 1800-1900* by Christy Kerins, Dublin 2000.
Ballybrown:	*A corner of Limerick) – history recollections and photography* by John Sheehan, Limerick 1995

Ballysteen: *Ballysteen the people and the place* by John M.
                         Feheney, Cork: Iverus Publications 1998

Bruff: A History of Bruff and district by Pius J.A. Browne,
                         M.A. thesis 1976-78 (UCC)
                         From Bruree to Corcomohide by Mainchin Seoighe,
                         Bruree/Rockhill Dev. Association 2000
Cappamore: *Cappamore- a parish history,* Cappamore Historical
                         Society and FAS 1992
Castleconnell: *The Annals of Castleconnell and Ahane since
                         prehistoric times* by John T. Gilhooly Limerick 1988.
                         'Castleconnell and its spa' by Robert Herbert in
                         NMAJ 1948 5 (4) p. 117-139:
                         Village by the Shannon –the story of Castleconnell, Joe
                         Carroll & Pat Tuohy published Limerick, Intype 1991.
Donoughmore: *An antique and storied land-a history of the parish of
                         Donoughmore, Knockea, Roxborough Co.Limerick
                         and its environs* by Thomas Toomey and Harry
                         Greensmyth, Limerick 1991
Doon: *Dun Bleisce* by Cumann Forbartha Dun Bleisce [edited
                         by G. Carew-Hynes], Limerick 1990.
Dromin-Athlacca: *Dromin Athlacca-the story of a rural parish in
                         Co.Limerick* by Mainchin Seoighe, Ath Leacach 1978
Glenroe: *Glenroe-Ballyorgan Parish - God's Acre* 1997
                         published by Glenroe-Ballyorgan Grave Committee.
Glin: *Glin Industrial School 1893-1973* by Christina Craft
                         1998. *The Knights of Glin* by John Anthony Gaughan,
                         Dublin, 1978.
Hospital: *A History of Hospital and its environs* by M.F.
                         O'Sullivan published Limerick 1995
Kenry: *Kenry the story of a barony in Co.Limerick* by Mairtin
                         O Corrbui, Dundalgan Press 1975
Kilmallock: *The story of Kilmallock* by Mainchin Seoighe,
                         Kilmallock Historical Society 1987
                         Kilmallock by Rev.James Dowd in JRHAAI , 1889, p.
                         204-15
Kilmurry: *A history of Kilmurry 1891-1991* edited by Pat
                         Holohan, Limerick 1991
Limerick: *Anatomy of a siege-King John's Castle 1642* by
                         Kenneth Wiggins, Wicklow Wordwell 2000
                         The Limerick Anthology edited by Jim Kemmy,
                         Dublin, Gill & McMillan 1996.
                         The Antiquities of Limerick and its neighbourhood by
                         T.J.Westropp, Dublin, Hodges Figgis 1916.

The Black Book of Limerick by Rev. James MacCaffrey, Dublin; Gill & Son 1907

The Building of Limerick by Judith Hill, Cork, Mercier Press, 1991

The Diocese of Limerick by Rev.John Begley, Dublin Browne & Nolan 1906 3 vols. reprinted O'Brien/Toomey publishers Limerick in 1993

Dowd's History of Limerick edited by Cian O'Carroll, Dublin, O'Brien Press 1990

Exploring Limerick's Past –an historical geography of urban development in County and City by Patrick J.O'Connor, Newcastle-West, Oireacht na Mumhan 1987

Georgian Limerick 1714 -1845 edited by David Lee and Bob Kelly, Limerick FAS/Limerick Civic Trust 1997; Vol.2 ed. David Lee & Christine Gonzalez 2000;

An history of the City of Limerick by John Ferrar 1767.

History of Limerick by Rev. P. Fitzgerald and J.J. McGregor Dublin, McKern 1826; republished 1999 O'Brien Books Limerick

History of Limerick by Maurice Lenihan, Limerick 1866. Facsimile edition by Cian O'Carroll, Cork, Mercier Press 1991

The History of Limerick city by Sean Spellissy, Limerick Celtic Bookshop 1998

Rev.Michael Moloney's 'How Limerick Came to be' in NMAJ, 1959 8, (2) (1959) p. 64-78

The Limerick Compendium edited by Jim Kemmy, Dublin, Gill & McMillan 1997

Limerick Historical Reflections by Kevin Hannon, Limerick, Oireacht Publications 1996

Limericks Fighting Story by J.M. MacCarthy, Tralee Anvil Books

Limerick the rich land by Sean Spellissy and John O'Brien,* Ennis, 1989.

Portrait of Limerick by Mainchin Seoighe, London Hale 1972

Remembering Limerick –historical essays celebrating the 800th. Anniversary of Limericks first charter granted in 1197 edited by David Lee, Limerick Civic Trust and FAS 1997

Reminiscences of Old Limerick. E.H. Bennis, Tralee, 3rd Ed. 1951

'Recent Research in Limerick City' by C. O'Rahilly, in *Arch. Irel.* 1988, 2   p 140-144.

'Recent Research in Limerick City.' J. Bradley. in
Arch. Irel. 1991 5 (3) p.25-28

Loughill/   *Recollections of our native valley-a history of*
Ballynahill: *Loughill-Ballyhahill* by Gerard Curtin, Loughill-
                        Ballyhahill Heritage Society, 1996

Monaleen: *The hidden excitement of Monaleen and Milford* by
                        Gerard Healy, Limerick Pallas publications 1991

Murroe: *Murroe and Boher –the history of an Irish country
                        parish* by Dom. Mark Tierney, Dublin Browne &
                        Nolan 1966

Parteen: *The history and folklore of Parteen and Meelick*
                        by Donal O'Riain and Seamas O'Cinneide, 1991,
                        Limerick

Pallaskenry: *Exploring Pallaskenry's past* – a journal of local
                        history by Fr. Martin McCormack, Pallaskenry 1995.

Patrickswell: *In the barony of Pubblebrien, Patrickswell and
                        Crecora, history of a Co.Limerick village and its
                        environs* by Gerard Beggan Galway 1990.

Rathkeale: *All Ireland is in and about Rathkeale* by P.J. O'Connor,
                        Newcastle-West, Oireacht na Mumhan 1996

If you have West Limerick roots you should visit www.asduchasdochas.pro.ie
for information on the history and folklore of this area. As Duchas Dochas is
the body set up under the auspices of Limerick county council which records
the lives of people in the West Limerick area.

12.3   Local History Journals

Several parish journals are published on a yearly basis with articles on the
history and antiquities of the surrounding areas. There is a large number of
amateur local historians throughout the county who dedicate themselves
to recording   details about their own areas. Although they are amateurs the
standard of their research bears testimony to their scholarship and dedication.
The Kilmallock Journal for example is edited by Dr. Mainchin Seoighe,
Limerick's most senior and highly respected historian. Tom Donovan co-
editor of the *Old Limerick Journal* also edits *The Ballybrown Journal* which
covers the Kilkeedy Clarina and Ballybrown areas near Limerick. There is a
good geographical spread covered by these journals, Glin (Glencorbry) and
Newcastlewest are all in West Limerick. Central Limerick has journals such as
Crom Abu for Croom and *Lough Gur* journals. An Green covers the Pallasgreen
area in East Limerick as does *Bleisce* (Doon) and *Ceapach Mhor* (Cappamore).
Further information on these parish publications can be had from any Limerick
library. For the two learned journals – the *North Munster Antiquarian Journal*
and the *Old Limerick Journal* readers can write respectively to the Hon. Ed.

Thomond Archaeological Society, c/o Dept. of History, Mary Immaculate College, South Circular Road, Limerick; and Editor, Old Limerick Journal, c/o Kemmy Museum, Castle Lane, Limerick.

Local History Journals of Limerick

Athea parish Journal
Ballybrown Journal
Ballyguiltenane Rural Journal
Bleisce
Ceapach Mhor
Crom Abu
Glencorbry Chronicle
An Grean
Kilmallock Historical Journal
Knockaderry and Clouncagh Jnl
Knockfierna and District Journal
Lough Gur and District Journal
NewcastleWest Historical Society Jnl
North Munster Antiquarian Journal
Old Limerick Journal
Pobblebrien Historical Jnl (Mungret area)

THE LOUGH GUR & DISTRICT
HISTORICAL SOCIETY
No4. 1988   JOURNAL

12.4   Other Miscellaneous Sources

Other useful sources include directories and other information on specific occupations in Limerick.

Croly's *Irish Medical Directory* of 1843 and 1846 lists the **medical** profession. 'Some Notable Limerick Doctors' in the NMAJ 1936 - 39, 1 (3) p. 113-123. See also the British Museum additional ms. 31885 *Entry book of Thomas Arthur M.D.* who practised in Limerick from 1619-1630. This includes a full list of patients and fees. It also contains information on the Arthur family and the history of Limerick.

Limerick **Church** of Ireland ministers are recorded in the *Irish Ecclesiastical Register* for the years 1817, 1818 and 1824. 'The Episcopal Succession of Killaloe' by Dermot Gleeson in NMAJ 1940/41, 2 (2) p. 51-62 lists Roman Catholic bishops from 1317-1616; There are lists of Roman Catholic priests and their parishes in the diocese of Cashel and Emly for 1836 and 1846. These are transcribed on the 'From Ireland' website –*www.from-ireland.net/ contents/limerickconts.htm*

The Glencorbry Chronicle

Published by
Glin Historical Society
Volume 1, No. 1

£5.00

Books and articles on Limerick **businesses** are less common. However, Limerick bankers are dealt with in *The old private banks and bankers of Munster, Part 1 Bankers of Cork and Limerick* by Eoin O'Kelly, CUP, 1959. Limerick family businesses are also noted in an article on 'Shop-signs of Eighteenth Century Limerick' by Robert Herbert in the NMAJ 1941 2 (4) p. 156-166

'Some trade guilds of Limerick' are in NMAJ 1941 2 (3) p. 121-134. 'The goldsmiths of Limerick' are in the NMAJ 1936-39 1 (4) p. 159-162. 'Mills and millers' by Dolly Stewart are in the OLJ 1980, 2, p. 22-23. 'Some Limerick Newsboys' are in the OLJ 1980 2, p. 40 and 1980 4, p. 31-32 . And Willie Gleeson has an article on printworkers in OLJ 1987, 21, p. 8. Morgan McCloskey deals with 'The coopers of Limerick – a craft of the past' in OLJ 1999, 36, p. 42-44.

The minute book of the Limerick guild of masons, bricklayers, slaters, plasterers, painters, pavours and lime-burners for the around the period June 1747 is in the NLI on microfilm N 5395.

If you are interested in an ancestor who was in the **police** (the Royal Irish Constabulary until 1921), you should consult *The Royal Irish Constabulary; a short history and genealogical guide,* Jim Herlihy, (Dublin 1997) for an account of the service and the records. The original records are in the British Library, but the NAI has microfilm copies of the personnel files. The LDS family history library also has these records (film no. 856057-69, 852088-852110).

British **Army** records are highly complex and are kept in various British Army archives depending on period of service, rank and regiment. See the *Guides to PRO and Army records for family historians* by S. Fowler, (London 1992). The LDS library has on microfiche the Limerick Royal Garrison Artillery Militia attestations, 1876-1911 which is an index of soldiers (with birthdates) serving in the militia – extracted from the Kew list, class WO96, pieces 1399-1401. There is a comprehensive *History of the Royal Munster Fusiliers* by McCance in two volumes (1652-1860, 1861-1922) republished in Cork by Schull Books 1995. As it includes the first world war period it is a useful source for Limerick men who joined during 1914 and 1918. Limerick City Library has *An alphabetical index to World War 1 casualties of the Royal Munster Fusiliers* by the Commonwealth War Graves Commission and also a list of casualties in the register listings of both World War 1 and 2.

A good introduction to **schools** and school records can be found in Michael V. Spillane's thesis on *Two centuries of popular education-an historical survey of the educational institutions of Limerick 1700-1900* (U.C.C. 1973).The county library holds a copy of this thesis. It has been supplemented by Mary Verling's recent thesis on education in Kilbehenny (U.C.C 1999) and by Sean McCarthy's 'The History of Schooling in Monagea 1834-1988' (typed copy held by Newcastlewest Library). 'Some schoolmasters in the diocese of Killaloe' by Rosemary ffolliott is in the NMAJ 1968, 11, p. 57-63. See also NLI ms.19,314 *a volume of short biographies of tutors and schoolmasters* dedicated to Lady Morgan and presented to her in Co.Limerick dated 1825.

Although the national (elementary) school system has been in existence since 1831 few records go back that far. You can however find a list of schools and schoolteachers for the Murroe –Boher area of county Limerick at *www.geocities.com/irishancestralpages/murbohlim.html* This lists Murroe, Clonkeen, Eyon and Kishiquirk national schools. Mainchin Seoighe's book *Dromin-Athlacca*, Athlacca, Co. Limerick 1978 lists schoolteachers for this parish and it also lists Catholic parish priests.

12.5 Travel Accounts

There are several narrative descriptions of both the city and county by travellers who visited Limerick in the 18th and 19th centuries. These give a flavour of life in the county in times past. These accounts can be very descriptive although one should be aware that they can sometimes give a jaundiced view. In 1752 Dr. Pococke for example had this to say about Limerick:

'All the rest of the town consists of narrow lanes, and it is a very dirty disagreeable place; Tho' so large there is not one good Inn where strangers can be well accommodated; they have a tavern indeed which has lodgings in it, commonly filled by officers: Both the air and water are looked on as unwholesome, and the army commonly lose many of their men here:'

Pococke's tour was followed by Arthur Young's *Tour In Ireland 1776-1779*. This was a much more detailed and objective account of this period. In 1834 H.D. Inglis published his *Ireland in 1834- a journey through Ireland during the Spring and Summer and Autumn of 1834*. J.G. John Forbes published his *Memorandums made in Ireland in the autumn of 1852*. Both of these works contain useful Limerick references.

12.6 Emigration and emigration sources

One of the most significant events of Irish emigration history was the Great Famine, which drove Irish people abroad. Between 1845 and 1921 at least 8 million people embarked for North America, Great Britain, Australia and New Zealand.
There is now a huge Irish diaspora abroad whose ancestors came from counties such as Limerick.

There are two very important publications that deal specifically with emigration from Limerick. These are *Poverty to Promise - the Monteagle emigrants 1838-58* by S.C. O'Mahony and Valerie Thompson, (Sydney, Crossing Press, 1994): *West Limerick Families Abroad* by Kate Press and Valerie Thompson published in Australia 2001. For emigration from a specific Limerick area consult S.C.O'Mahony's article 'Kilmallock workhouse emigration, 1848-60' in LGDJ 1987, p. 1-8. Many emigrants are also identified in O'Mahony's 'Emigration from the Limerick workhouse, 1848-1860' in *Ir. Anc.* 1982, 14, p. 83-94 and his article 'Emigration from Newcastle Union, 1848-1859' in *Jrnl. Newcastlewest Historical Society*, 2002, 3, p. 28-34.

Descendants of Limerick people are found scattered in all quarters of the globe although the principal destinations were Britain, North America, Australia and New Zealand. You are far more likely to find documentary evidence of an emigrant's arrival in one of these countries, than of their departure from Ireland. This is because there are hardly any original passenger lists in Irish archives, nor is there any register of those who emigrated. Movement between England, Scotland and Wales was also undocumented as Ireland was then part of the United Kingdom. There were no official records of emigrants created at the port of departure and very few records by shipping companies survive. Passenger lists do not usually give the place of origin of the emigrant and this diminishes their value as a genealogical source. Matters are further complicated by the fact that many Irish emigrants going to North America departed from Liverpool, so their first point of emigration from Ireland was to Britain.

In short, records of emigration tend to be better in the country of destination. U.S. records are quite good and Australian records, especially transportation and assisted passage emigrants, are a very valuable genealogical resource.

If you are searching for your Limerick ancestor from abroad begin with the sources in your own country and work backwards. Some useful approaches are:

a) Try to establish that your ancestors were actually from Limerick. Note that emigrants from Clare, Tipperary and Kerry also departed from Limerick port.
b) Try to identify, from records in your home country, the parish in which they lived in Ireland. Parish identification is very important as there was no county-wide index to births, marriages and deaths before 1864.
c) Where feasible, find out as much as you can from your oldest relatives. Check family memorabilia such as letters, diaries etc. Where possible you should check the gravestones of the original settlers. The more homework you do in your own country the better. Any bit of information may later prove to be the critical link with some Irish record source.
d) Obtain copies of death certificates (in your home country), of any ancestor born in Limerick as the place of birth may be noted. Also locate the citizenship or naturalisation record of the ancestor/ancestors concerned.

Microfilmed copies of passenger lists are in the U.S. National Archives and its regional centres. Under the 1819 Act to Regulate Passenger Ships, masters of vessels arriving at American ports had to submit lists of those carried. The lists included the name, age, occupation of all passengers, their home country, the name of the ship, port of embarkation, and the date of its arrival in port. The LDS also has these microfilms. Again in the U.S. one also should consult the indexes for persons crossing the border between the U.S. and Canada. Access to immigrant records during the famine period has improved in recent years with the publication of the seven volume *The Famine Immigrants; lists of Irish immigrants arriving at the port of New York 1846-1851* by Glazier and Tepper. This source is particularly useful where the surname is unusual or where the names of the family group emigrating are known. However the problem is that passengers entering the U.S. could have used other ports or entered via Canada. One should also take a look at *Filby's Passenger and Immigration Lists Index* which is an index to the published passenger lists. Brian Mitchell's book *Irish Passenger Lists 1803-06* lists passengers sailing from Ireland to America for that period. Patrick J. Blessing's *The Irish in America- a guide to the literature and the manuscript collections* gives useful information re: the sources available.

The **internet** is particularly useful for emigration sources. Passenger lists can be accessed at www.rootsweb.com/~fianna/migrate/index.html. This site has an Irish ships list and links to Cyndi's list –ships. There are also commercially released CD-ROM's containing scans of passenger lists. Broderbund Software has a CD-ROM for Irish Immigrants to North America 1803-1871. The address is *www.familytreemaker.com/immigran.html*
Some surviving passenger lists are available on the internet. At the ancestry section of www.irishtimes.com one can access lists for ships that departed from Limerick. A fee is charged for access. The ships listed are:
• Bryan Abbs destination New York in 1850.
• Constitution destination New Haven in 1821.
• Victoria destination New York in 1851.
• Columbine destination New York in 1852.(from U.S. National Archives film M237, reel 115, list 799).

At www.genealogy.org/~ajmorris there are listings for a number of ships that arrived in the U.S. carrying Irish passengers.
If your Limerick ancestor settled in **Canada** the national and territorial archives should prove useful. The Canadian National Archives has a booklet called 'Tracing Your Ancestors in Canada'. The book *Irish Emigrants to Canada 1839-47 from the Wyndham estates in Counties Clare, Limerick and Tipperary* by F. Leeson (listed at *Ancestry.com*) should be consulted.

In relation to **Australian** records the NAI holds a wide range of records relating to the transportation of convicts from Ireland to Australia in the period 1788 to 1868. In some cases these include records of convicts' families transported as free settlers. The *Transportation Records Database* gives an index and is on the internet at *www.nationalarchives.ie/search01.html* Readers should also consult Rena Lohan's work 'Sources in the National Archives to research into the transportation of Irish convicts to Australia 1791-1853' which is in the *Journal of the Irish Society for Archives,* Spring 1996. The excellent immigration records of assisted emigration to New South Wales have been indexed on computer for the 1848-70 period by Richard Reid and these are now available in repositories such as the Mitchell Library, NSW Archives, and the Society of Australian Genealogists, Sydney. The state archives of Victoria in Melbourne have indexed the Victorian collection manually. As most Australian records are held in the Archives of New South Wales, Tasmania Victoria and Western Australia these institutions can first be visited on the internet. The NSW Archives have produced a *Guide to Shipping and the Free Passenger Lists* and a *Guide to the Convict Records* .

There is a list of Irish convicts to New South Wales from 1791 to 1820 at *www.pcug.org.au/~ppmay/convicts.htm* This includes convicts whose trial took place in Limerick.

Also take a look at the book *Oceans of Consolation*-personal accounts of Irish migration to Australia by David Fitzpatrick, Cork, 1994

The seal of Limerick City
from *The Topographical Dictionary of Ireland* by Samuel Lewis (1837)

Chapter 13 Archives, Services and Addresses

This chapter provides a listing of the main holdings of the local and national repositories in Ireland. While the majority of repositories are located in Dublin, much research can be undertaken in Limerick.

Also listed are useful addresses, both postal and web site.

13.1 Limerick Repositories:

Limerick Ancestry, The Granary, Michael Street, Limerick. Ph.061 415125/ Fax.061 312985 *www.limerickancestry.com*

Limerick Ancestry is an official Heritage centre and is part of a national network set up in each county to index local records and offers a comprehensive search service for a fee. It is part of the Irish Family History Foundation which acts as the coordinating body for research centres in Ireland. It operated formerly as part of the Limerick Regional Archives. It is totally dedicated to ancestral research and has over one million Limerick records.

Its major holdings are:
- Catholic Church registers with start dates from 1745 to 1867
- Church of Ireland records with start dates from 1692 to 1893
- Presbyterian Church records from 1828
- Methodist records from 1824
- Civil records: non-Catholic marriage records from 1845
  Births, marriages and deaths from 1864
- Griffith's Valuation records
- Tithe Applotment Books 1824 - 1835
- 1901 and 1911 Census returns for Limerick City and County
- Newspapers and estate records, Gravestone inscriptions

Limerick Ancestry is recommended for carrying out commissioned research. While great enjoyment can be had from hunting records in various repositories, many researchers are constrained by time and distance from these sources of information. Commissioning research at Limerick Ancestry is a useful option. The staff are very familiar with the layout, content and idiosyncrasies of the sources. Their website provides a genealogical research form which you can submit with the basic details of your ancestors. All research is carried out for a fee. Visitors are welcome for consultations.

Limerick City Library, The Granary, Michael Street, Limerick. Ph.061 314668/ Fax.061 415906 e-mail:citylib@limerickcity.ie *www.limerickcorp.ie*

Limerick City Library has a large local studies section that holds books, journals and newspapers. This user friendly library has a dedicated member of staff to deal with queries.

Holdings include:
- Census records: 1901 returns(m/f) and 1911 returns(CD Rom).
- Land records: Tithe Applotment Books, Griffiths Primary Valuations.
- Memorial Inscriptions: Memorials of the Dead(12 volumes and surname index for 1888-1909), Ireland's Memorial Records 1914-1918(WWI).
- Miscellaneous: Collection of newspapers, Directories, Family Histories and a collection of items relating to Limerick history.
- Voters lists for Limerick City from 1923.

Limerick County Library, 59 O'Connell Street, Limerick. Ph.061 214452/ 318447/Fax.061 318570 e-mail:libinfo@limerickcoco.ie *www.lcc.ie*
This library's collection of books and journals has a particular emphasis on publications dealing with the history and antiquities of Limerick County.
Holdings include:
- Census records: Civil Survey of 1654, Pender's Census of 1659, 1901 and 1911 returns(CD Rom).
- Land records: Tithe Applotment Books, Griffiths Primary Valuations.
- Miscellaneous: Grand Jury Presentments 1811-1900, Family Histories, Lewis's *Topographical Dictionary for Limerick*(available on the Limerick County Council web site at *www.lcc.ie*).

Palatine Museum, Rathkeale, Co. Limerick. Ph.069 64397/Fax.069 64220 e-mail: ipass@eircom.net
The Irish Palatine Heritage Centre is operated by Austin Bovenizer and is open during the summer months and off-season by appointment. Opening times are Sundays 2pm –5pm; Tuesday –Friday 10am –1pm and 2pm – 5pm. The Irish Roots magazine has profiled this heritage centre in its 1996 edition. There is also a good guide to the museum on the web at *www. irishpalatines.org/ heritagecentre.html*

Superintendent Registrar's Office,
There are two such offices serving Limerick city and county respectively, each of which has birth, marriage and death records from 1864. If you are researching a city ancestor then go to St. Camillus Hospital, Shelbourne Road(off the Ennis Road)Limerick. Ph.061 483763/Fax.061 483767. If on the other hand you are looking for a county record then you need to go to St.Ita's Hospital, Gortboy, NewcastleWest, Co. Limerick. Ph.069 62545/Fax.069 62980. There are no search rooms available but certificates can be obtained for known births etc.

Tipperary Heritage Unit, The Bridewell, St. Michael Street, Limerick. Ph./ Fax.062 52725 e-mail: thu@iol.ie
This centre is the authorised research unit for Catholic Records of the RC

Diocese of Cashel and Emly and as such concentrates most of its work in Co. Tipperary. However much of east Limerick also falls within its remit (see list of RC parishes in chapter 5, the relevant parishes are those followed by the letters EM). They have indexed the baptismal and marriage records. A search service is provided for a fee.

13.2 Dublin Repositories

Dublin has the major national repositories of records necessary to do research on Limerick ancestors. The most important are the General Register Office, the National Archives, the National Library of Ireland, the Valuation Office and the Registry of Deeds.

General Register Office, Joyce House, 8-11 Lombard Street East, Dublin 2. Ph.01 6711000/Fax.01 6711243 *www.groireland.ie*
This is the central repository for records relating to births, marriages and deaths in the Republic of Ireland. Although the office does not carry out genealogical research it provides research facilities for those who wish to do so. A search of the indexes (5 consecutive years at a time) for a specific entry can be undertaken. Full details of the procedure and costs are available on the GRO website.
The indexes are organised by name, and year (or quarter) and District (see chapter 6 Civil Registration). The index will provide a reference number with which you can request a copy of the entry (see p.60). To efficiently conduct a search you should have a reasonable idea of the location and time of the event, and also be aware of possible name variants that should also be searched.
You may also request a copy of a certificate by mail or e-mail. In order to do this you will need to have sufficient information i.e. full name, date of birth, place of birth. It can also be useful to have other details to verify that the cert provided is the correct one (e.g. surname of mother, full name of father etc.).

The National Archives, Bishop Street, Dublin 8. Ph.01 4072300/Fax.01 4072333. e-mail: mail@nationalarchives.ie *www.nationalarchives.ie*
The National Archives is the major repository for documents generated by State and public organisations. It is an amalgamation of several older repositories including the Public Record Office and the State Paper Office. It mainly holds official government papers, but also papers that have been donated by other organizations and individuals. The major holdings are the 1901 and 1911 census returns; Griffith's Valuation; the Tithe Applotment Books, wills and administrations. An introduction to the genealogical records is available at: *www.nationalarchives.ie/genealogy.html* For those who plan a visit, there is an excellent Reading Room. A short pamphlet entitled 'Sources for Family History and Genealogy' may be consulted as a preliminary step and

is also on the website. You must request and specify each item so it will save time if you have identified exactly what you want to view in advance. It can be slow researching some of the material as it comes in an unwieldy format such as in boxes or in files tied in bundles. Copies of specific items can be requested by mail.   Just recently the NAI has launched a new genealogy service which is available to the public from Monday to Friday from 10.00 am until 5.00 pm. For further information on this service check the NAI website (see above). The website also lists researchers who will conduct research on your behalf.

The National Library, Kildare Street, Dublin 2. Ph.01 60302000/Fax.01 6766690 e-mail: info@nli.ie *www.nli.ie*
It behoves all of us at some time or another to visit this wonderful treasure house of history, literature and culture. It mainly holds privately published materials such as books, newspapers, pamphlets, directories, journals and histories, but also church records, Griffith's Valuation and the Tithe Applotment Books. It also has extensive collections of maps, manuscripts estate papers and photographs. Its Genealogical Advisory Service can direct you on how to go about family history research and direct you to relevant sources.   They also hold the best collection of microfilmed Roman Catholic Church registers (see chapter 5; Church Records).   The library's website at www.nli.ie should first be explored as it has an excellent introduction on getting started on the registers, and can help to identify the particular one of relevance to you. In this way you can do some of the essential groundwork before you make a visit or request a researcher to do so on your behalf. A list of such researchers is also available on the website. Note: a valid identification is necessary when making a visit and an application form for a reader's ticket is available at the website

The Genealogical Office, 2 Kildare Street, Dublin 2. Ph.01 60203000/Fax01 676690 e-mail: herald@nli.ie *www.nli.ie*
The Genealogical Office is now part of the National Library of Ireland. Most of their records relate to the analysis or authentication of pedigrees, such as a grant of arms, confirmation of arms and the registration of pedigrees. The bulk of such records relate to Anglo-Irish families. Those pedigrees listed in *Hayes Manuscript Sources* (see chapter 11) are normally available to the public. Many of the GO manuscripts have been microfilmed and are available in the LDS and in the National Library. Others may be consulted by visiting the Manuscript reading room at the Genealogical Office. A manuscript reading room ticket may be applied for in the National Library. For a full account of this source of information readers are referred to John Grenham's *Tracing Your Irish Ancestors.*

Registry of Deeds, Henrietta Street, Dublin 1. Ph.01 6707500
e-mail: webmaster@landregistry *www.irlgov.ie/landreg/*
The Registry of Deeds holds deeds (see chapter 3 Land Records) from 1708

to the present, all of which are accessible to the general public. For a nominal fee you can spend the day exploring its indexes and transcripts. The system of indexes, and of documentation, is complex and the website is a good starting point for visitors.

The Representative Church Body Library, Braemor Park, Churchtown, Dublin 14. Ph.01 4923979 / Fax.01 49245770 *www.ireland.anglican.org/ home.html*
This library is the chief reference library and repository of the Church of Ireland. It holds the largest single collection of Church of Ireland parish registers as well as vestry books, preachers' books and account books. A listing of all the church registers held can be purchased. In certain cases you may have to get permission to view some of the records held. Check with the RCBL before you visit. Certified copies of entries in the registers can also be issued. Note that photocopying from the parish records can only be undertaken with the written permission of the owner of the copyright. The staff on duty will assist you with this matter. The RCBL also has an extensive collection of biographical information on C of I clergymen. An account of the range of Church of Ireland records is provided by the RCBL librarian, Dr. Raymond Refausse in chapter 3 of *Irish Church Records* edited by James G.Ryan (Flyleaf Press, 2001) (see 5.2).

Valuation Office, Irish Life Centre, Abbey Street lower, Dublin 1. Ph.01 8171000/Fax.01 8171180 e-mail: info@valoff.ie *www.valoff.ie*
This office holds the records relating to the system of land valuation which is still used to determine local taxation. It holds the records of valuation of all properties, and the valuation maps for the country from 1846. Details held in relation to each property are, occupier name, townland address, description of property, acreage of holding, rateable value and reference to its position on a valuation map. Valuation maps are also archived and can therefore locate the position of a property back to c. 1850. The records in the Valuation Office can be searched for a fee, and copies can also be provided. There is a genealogy link on the website of the Valuation Office which is a useful starting point for anyone interested in making a visit.

Family History Libraries (LDS)
Followers of the Church of Jesus Christ of Latter-day Saints (the Mormons) believe that their ancestors may become posthumous members of their church. As a consequence of this belief the Mormons have a huge interest in genealogy. Their Family History Library was established in Salt Lake City, Utah, U.S.A. in 1894. It has become the largest library of its kind in the world. Filming of Irish records began in 1948 and the current collection amounts to over 10,000 reels of film.
The Family History Library Catalogue is held in every family history centre

and lists the records held in the forms of books, microfilms, microfiches or CD-ROM. It is essential to check this catalogue first for a description of their holdings. It is at: www.familysearch.org/eng/Library/FHLC/frameset_ fhlc.asp. There are Family History Centres in Dublin, Cork, and in Limerick city. The Limerick Family History Centre is at the Latter Day Saints church on the Dooradoyle Road. They hold the1901 census, index to births 1864-1921, marriages 1845-1921, and deaths 1864-1921. Other microfilms can be ordered from the main library on short loan.

The centres also hold the International Genealogical Index (IGI). This is a worldwide index of births, baptisms, marriages and deaths compiled from various sources and although it is not a comprehensive collection it is worth consulting. The names are listed alphabetically county by county, and country by country indexes. There are over a million entries for Ireland but note that they are not joined in family groups or pedigrees.

Useful Addresses

Churches:

Roman Catholic
Archdiocese of Cashel and Emly,
Archbishop's House, Thurles,
Co. Tipperary
Tel. 0504 21512 Fax 0504 22680
e-mail; cashelemly@eircom.net

Diocese of Killaloe,
Diocesan Office, Westbourne,
Ennis, Co.Clare
Tel. 065 6828638 Fax 065 6842538
e-mail; cildalua@iol.ie

Diocese of Limerick,
Diocesan Office,
66 O'Connell St, Limerick
Tel. 061 315856 Fax 061310186
e-mail; diocoff@eircom.net
www.limerick-diocese.org/

Church of Ireland
Bishop's House, North Circular
Road, Limerick
Tel. 061 451532 Fax 061451100
e-mail bishop@limerick.anglican.
org

Church of Ireland diocesan
Secretary,
St. Cronan's Rectory, Roscrea,
Co.Tipperary
Tel. 0505 21725 Fax 0505 21993
e-mail; condell@iol.ie

Presbyterian
United Presbyterian and Methodist
Church:
Rev. David A. Range,
Clonmacken, Ennis Road, Limerick
Tel. 061 325325

Presbyterian Historical Society of Ireland
Church House,
Fisherwick Place,
Belfast BT1 6DW
Northern Ireland
http://www.presbyterianireland.org

Northern Ireland
Public Record Office of Northern Ireland
66 Balmoral Avenue,
Belfast BT9 6NY
Northern Ireland
http://proni.nics.gov.uk/index.htm

Rathkeale/Newcastle Family Roots by Noel Farrell (Longford 2002)
includes listings for the 1901 & 1911 census returns,
Griffiths Valuations and the Electors Register for 1940 for these areas.

Index

NOTES

NOTES

NOTES

NOTES

NOTES

NOTES

NOTES